PRESS NOTICES – 1912

From the **SCOTSMAN:** "To this book must be given a high place among the literature of travel and adventure. . . . It shows how truth can be more interesting than fiction . . . . In it there is much that is interesting about New Zealand, the gold fields, trading, whaling, and sealing expeditions in the Pacific, shipwreck and life on a desert island, the furthest South inhabitants of the planet, etc.' . . . . From the observations on some of the deeper problems of life that are interspersed in the narrative it is evident that Mr Inches Thomson is a man of thought as well as action."

From the **FREEMAN'S JOURNAL:** "A new book of travels that is equal to some of Frank Bullen's work in sincerity and charm. His description of the wreck of the *Bencleugh* on Macquarie Island would take a deal of beating for its picturesque and vivid power."

From the **ATHENAEUM:** "Interesting reminiscences of an old Colonial."

From the **PERTHSHIRE PAPERS:** "A fascinating book with several fine photo reproductions. . . . Mr Thomson is to be congratulated on the exceedingly able manner in which he has handled his subject, and his volume should prove a welcome addition to many a library."

From the **Sydney Morning Herald:** "The record of his adventures is set forth in "Voyages and Wanderings in Far-off Seas and Lands," and though the author would hardly claim to be possessed of all the airs and graces of literary craftsmanship, he has contrived to write a very readable book about an eventful career.

From **E.G.T.:** "Wanderings and voyages are just delightful. I have not had such a treat since I read 'Robinson Crusoe' a long, long time ago."

VERY SUITABLE FOR SCHOOL PRIZES.
HEADLEY BROTHERS, BISHOPSGATE, LONDON

First published 1912
by Headley Brothers, Bishopsgate. (London)

This edition published 2023
by Wonderful World Ltd. (NZ)
With additional material
Copyright © 2023 Rosy Fenwicke

This fully annotated edition of *Voyages and Wanderings in Far-off Seas and Lands* includes; explanations of historical context, maps and illustrations of objects and places mentioned in the original version, and additional information about John Thomson's life.

ISBN: 978-1-9911942-0-6
eISBN: 978-1-9911942-1-3
POD ISBN: 978-1-9911942-2-0

A catalogue record for this book is available from the
National Library of New Zealand

www.rosyfenwickeauthor.com
Wonderful World Ltd.

Images copyright © as credited 2023

Cover design by Amanda Sutcliffe
Design & layout www.yourbooks.co.nz

VOYAGES
and WANDERINGS
in FAR-OFF SEAS
and LANDS

Illustrated, Annotated Version

J. INCHES THOMSON

INTRODUCTION BY ROSY FENWICKE

INTRODUCTION

Ka u ki Mata-nuku,
Ka u ki Mata-rangi;
Ka u ki tēnei whenua.
Hei whenua.
Mau e kai te manawa o tauhou.
[I come where a new land is under my foot,
Where a new sky is over my head;
Here on this new land I stand
A home for me,
O spirit of the Earth! The stranger offers his heart to thee!]

Māori karakia on arriving in a strange country.[1]

---

1   New Zealand or Ao-Teā-Roa: (The Long Bright World). Its Wealth and
     Resources, Scenery, Travel-Routes, Spas and Sport, by James Cowan. Publisher:
     New Zealand Government Department of Tourist and Health Resorts. 1908.

An early geographer once described New Zealand as a 'land without people waiting for a people without land.'[2]

Six hundred and eighty million years ago, it had been part of the Gondwana supercontinent, which then separated to become New Zealand, Australia, Africa, South America, Antarctica, and the subcontinent of India. New Zealand lacked land mammals other than a few species of small bat, but its ecosystem surrounded by 18,000 km of coastline hosting fish, shellfish, seabirds and marine mammals, would develop over 82 million years into what would be called a 'larder of protein.'[3]

The first humans arrived here in the mid-thirteenth century. Their ancestors had colonised East and West Polynesia, island hopping across the Pacific 5000 to 6000 years earlier from the mainland of South East Asia, using the stars and ocean currents for navigation in canoes stabilised with outriggers, powered by sail. There is evidence that by the first millennium of the Christian era, these Austronesians were making 'extraordinarily widespread return voyages throughout the Central and South Pacific'.[4] An initial settlement of New Zealand of between 100 to 200 people was required for the Māori population to increase to between 100,000 and 110,00 people as it had by the eighteenth century.[5] Most had journeyed from East rather than West Polynesia and, in particular, the Society, Marquesas, Astral and Cook groups.[6]

For unknown reasons, return journeys and further exploration stopped after the thirteen century, and for the next four hundred years, Māori flourished in complete isolation from the rest of the world. The

2   The Penguin History of New Zealand by Michael King. 2003. Penguin Books
3   Ibid
4   Ibid
5   Ibid
6   Ibid

culture of Te Ao Māori, based upon but distinct from their Polynesian forebears, became embedded in the people and their places in the land. Passed down by oral tradition, Te Ao Māori was reinforced at familial (hapū) and tribal (iwi) levels by the survivors and thus they and their customs are those that are remembered.

Māori named the South Island, Te Wai Pounamu meaning the waters of greenstone. It was settled when northern tribes travelled south to harvest seafood and search for pounamu. Ngāti Mamoe from Ahūriri (Napier) settled the Kaikoura coast by conquering and absorbing the earlier inhabitants, the Waitaha. Chiefs of what would become Ngāi Tahu arrived from the eastern North Island, (Te Ika ā Māui), mainly from the Ngāti Porou and Ngāti Kahungunu tribes.[7] By the seventeenth century, many pā or fortified villages had been established to secure positions along the East Coast of the South Island for summer fishing expeditions with the principal Ngāi Tahu settlement based at Kaiapoi north of what is now Christchurch. In summer, the villages were hives of industry as people gathered and prepared food to carry them through the rest of the year before retreating to warmer northern regions in winter.

Seafarers born two oceans and twelve thousand miles away interrupted the isolation of Māori, first in 1642 and later in the 1770s. After the sightings by Tasman and the landings by Cook, contact became more frequent. In the years leading up to 1840 European sailors, many of whom had been convicts, jumped ship to settle in New Zealand. These men took Māori wives, had Māori children and lived according to Māori custom becoming what were called Pākeha Māori.

---

7   Te Wai Pounamu: The Greenstone Island. A History of the Southern Māori during the European Colonization of New Zealand by H. C. Evison. Aoraki Press. 1993.

In 1822, one of the first European visitors to Te Wai Pounamu observed playful children, men and women living to advanced old ages (80-95), and well-constructed houses with raised floors, and canoes of varying length, depending on their purpose. Designated war canoes were 70 to 100 feet, making fast travel along the coast possible. He also noted these canoes were only stable in calm seas, and that Māori quickly came to appreciate the greater seaworthiness of whale boats.[8]

Visits by European ships were welcome as Māori traded flax, and potatoes (brought to New Zealand by Captain Cook in 1776) for metal goods such as nails, cooking implements, and later weapons. However, there were several incidents when sailors were perceived to have given offence and were quickly killed, cooked, and eaten. In Sydney, this gave Māori a reputation for being 'generally fierce and cruel.'[9] Retaliation from Europeans could be equally merciless. In 1817 Captain Kelly from the *Sophia* killed over 50 Māori and destroyed an entire village after Māori killed three of his sailors. (see footnote page 28).

Undeterred, the sealers and whalers kept coming. By the late 1820s, whaling had replaced sealing as the seals had been all but exterminated from coastal New Zealand. The whaling industry grew rapidly to meet the Northern hemisphere's demand for oil to lubricate machinery and to light homes. Candles were made from spermaceti from inside the whale's skull, and from oil which was extracted from the blubber. Without whale oil, an excellent lubricant, the Industrial Revolution would not have been possible. Whalebone and baleen were used in clothing and other items which today are made from plastic.

In 1826, J. Shepherd visiting on the ship Rosanna described Ōtākou harbour thus, 'bird life was prolific, fish were plentiful and within the

---

8   Ibid.
9   Ibid.

harbour itself were seen a number of whales'.[10]

The Ngāi Tahu peoples of Murihiku, Ōtākou and Kaiapoi, increasingly vied for dominance when trading with Europeans. This was despite a unifying ariki (aristocracy) class, responsible for maintaining the peace and upholding the mana of the noble line, having built up over many generations of intermarriage between prominent families of Ngāi Tahu and Ngāti Mamoe. Te Hau Tapunuiota, a prominent eighteenth century Ngāi Tahu chief is the ancestor of those who would contribute most to the history of the tribe in the nineteenth century. His son Hōnekai, his grandsons, Te Whakataupuka, and Te Maiharanui and his great grandson Tūhawaiki became respected warriors and powerful leaders in the fight against incursions by Ngāti Toa during the southern Musket Wars. In 1844, Tūhawaiki was one of twenty-five signatories to the Ōtākou Settlement purchase.

Resource-rich Te Wai Pounamu had not gone unnoticed by northern tribes and in 1828 Ngāti Toa based on the West Coast of the North Island, mounted a raiding party on Ngāi Tahu which culminated in the death at Kaiapoi, of the famous Ngāti Toa chief, Te Pēhi. Ngāti Toa withdrew but returned during each fighting season for the next five years. Armed with muskets and led by Te Rauparaha, they set about decimating the population of Ngāi Tahu, who were then still relying on traditional weapons and strategies for war.

In the fighting season of 1833, Tūhawaiki and four prominent Ngāi Tahu chiefs, Te Whakataupuka, Karetai, Taiarioa and Haereroa decided to oust Ngāti Tōa and Te Rauparaha from Te Wai Pounamu once and for all. Their taua sailed north from Ōtākou with 700 warriors in 30 war

---

10   Contributions to the Early History of New Zealand. [Settlement of Otago], by Thomas Moreland Hocken. 1898. Sampson Low, Marston and Company, St Dunstan's House, Fetter Lane, Fleet Street, London EC.

canoes and whaleboats. They destroyed the whaling station owned by Te Rauparaha at Cloudy Bay, killing both Māori and Europeans and ending Ngāti Tōa's occupation of Te Wai Pounamu.

Retaliation never came because when Karetai and his wife Tipu returned from Sydney in 1834 they were both infected with measles. Te Whakataupuka died, and the disease spread up the island infecting and killing half the population before crossing the strait and killing many North Island Māori.

In 1836, John Jones' schooner the *Sydney Packet* brought tuberculosis to Ōtākou. By the end of that year, it was estimated half the Māori population had died of three European diseases; measles, influenza and tuberculosis. With fewer labourers, the flax and potato harvests suffered, there was less trade and what had been a thriving economy withered, further weakening an already vulnerable Ngāi Tahu tribe.

Shore based whaling stations provided some employment in winter, allowing those left to undertake the seasonal harvests in summer. Weller's station at Ōtākou employed 85 men in 1835, one quarter of whom were Māori. By 1839, half of the employees were Māori. Johnny Jones employed 280 men at his seven shore whaling stations in 1839, many of whom were Māori.[11]

In 1838, news reached Sydney that the British government would annex New Zealand. This led to a flurry of acquisitions of land titles of shore based stations. That year, the *Magnet* arrived in Sydney with Tūhawaiki, Taiaroa, Karetai, Topi Patuki and Haereroa on board. The five chiefs sold vast tracks of land to Johnny Jones and his fellow

---

11   The Welcome of Strangers. An Ethnohistory of Southern Māori 16-50-1850, by
        Atholl Anderson. 1998. Otago University Press.

merchants Green, Small and Peake.[12] In February Taiaroa went back to Sydney and sold even more land. The money raised from the land sales meant Tūhawaiki and his peers could purchase the weapons to arm themselves against future threats from Te Rauparaha. After the Treaty of Waitangi was signed in 1840, the 'Queen's Peace' prevailed and there were no more fighting seasons.

In 1843-44 the Māori population was estimated to be between 1500 and 2000. This was down from the population estimated to be between 3000 and 4000 in 1820. Disease, Ngāti Tōa and intermarriage contributed to this decline. [13]

In 1843 on the other side of the world, George Rennie, a liberal Scottish politician and sculptor, and Captain William Cargill promoted the establishment of a 'New Edinburgh' preferably in the Middle Island 'with its freedom from native troubles, its more suitable climate and grain-producing soil.'[14] The settlement would have a special Scottish character, was to be established by the New Zealand Company and therefore was to be organised on the Company principles of systematic colonisation.

The Company despatched the surveyor, Frederick Tuckett from Nelson in the South Island along with two companions to undertake the survey and recommend a suitable site. A member of the surveying expedition, David Monro, wrote this description of the lower Ōtākou Harbour. 'The weather, while we lay in Otago, was beautiful. The sky, the great part of the time, was without a cloud, and not a breeze ruffled the surface of the water, which reflected the surrounding

12   Te Wai Pounamu: The Greenstone Island. A History of the Southern Māori during the European Colonization of New Zealand, H. C. Evison. 1993. Aoraki Press.

13   Ibid: The Welcome of Strangers.

14   Hocken.

wooded slopes and every sea-bird that floated upon it, with mirror-like accuracy. For some hours after sunrise, the woods resounded with the rich and infinitely varied notes of thousands of tuis and other songsters.'[15]

The trees referred to included red pine or rimu, black pine or matai, miro, rata, totara and in certain areas at the head of the harbour, white pine or kahikatea, interlaced with bush lawyers and supplejacks and all protected by a dense and tangled undergrowth down to the sea. Along the harbour were 'luxuriant masses of ferns, mosses and lichens'. The silver tree fern was abundant on the peninsula. Further diversity was provided by native flax, dwarf shrubs, grasses and the like. "So dense was this rich cover which seemed like a natural barrier to man's intrusion" that in 1844 when Tuckett approached the Harbour from the north, he found the forest along the Mihiwaka-Cargill-Flagstaff ridge of an almost impenetrable character.[16]

Despite the density of the bush, Mr Tuckett decided Ōtākou would make a better site for settlement than Port Levy near Lyttleton. Tūhawaiki and Taiaroa had backed the Port Levy location and were waiting there to negotiate the land sale. On hearing the news that Ōtepoti at the head of Ōtākou harbour was the recommended option, they sent word to Murihiku that a sale was imminent. Within two days, eighteen boats carrying 150 members of Ngāi Tāhu arrived at Kōpūtai (Port Chalmers).

In mid-July 1844, Captain Wakefield of the New Zealand Company arrived from Wellington to discuss the purchase of 200,000 acres. Land was to be set aside for Ngāi Tahu at the end of Ōtākou peninsula, where

---

15   The Port of Otago by A.H. McLintock. 1951. Whitcombe and Tombs.
16   Ibid.

the principle kāinga (villages) and urupā (burial grounds) were situated. The price negotiated for 200,000 acres was £2400. This amount was justified on the basis that the land retained by Māori would increase in value as a result of European development.

Twenty-five chiefs including Tūhawaiki, Taiaroa and Karetai signed the deed of purchase of the Ōtākou Block with the New Zealand Company on the 31st of July 1844 on the foreshore at Kōpūtai.

They were well aware of the implication of selling land to Europeans in this way, as evidenced by a speech Karetai gave to his people in which he explained that the land would transfer to European ownership and Ngāi Tahu occupation would cease.[17]

However due to another reversal in the fortunes of the New Zealand Company, it wasn't until 1848 that the first settlers arrived on board the *John Wickliffe* and the *Phillip Laing* to take up the land.

In the mid-nineteenth century, 'the preferred destination for British and Irish migrants was North America, followed by Australia. From 1810 to 1860, the number of settlers in Australasia shot up from 12,000 to 1.25 million, expanding a hundredfold in fifty years.'[18] The settlers didn't come to colonise and subjugate. They came because there were opportunities in New Zealand not available in their impoverished, overpopulated and class-ridden home countries - likely the same reasons which had propelled the Austronesians to explore and settle first in the Pacific and then New Zealand. James Belich put it like this. 'Settlers wanted a life as well as a living. What is more, they were not ogres. They were whining bundles of hopes and fears, just like us.'[19]

17   Ibid. Evison.
18   Colonialism: A Moral Reckoning, by Nigel Biggar. 2023. William Collins Books.
      HarperCollins Publishers.
19   Replenishing the Earth: The Settler Revolution and the Rise of the Anglo-World,

John Sen Inches Thomson (1844-1933) was neither impoverished nor down-trodden but like his forebears he sought adventure, novelty, commercial success and new frontiers. His father Captain Watson Thomson spent his life at sea until in 1837 he settled in Alloa, Clackmannanshire, Scotland, married Jane Brown and had three children; Janet (1838), Andrew (1841), and John (1844).

Alloa in the Central Lowlands of Scotland is situated on the North bank of the Forth River where is becomes the Firth of the Forth. In the eighteenth and nineteenth centuries it was a thriving river port from where the manufactured goods of southern Scotland were exported to the continent. Daniel Defoe said of the town 'At Alloa... a merchant may trade to all parts of the world.' By the middle of the twentieth century the ships had outgrown the river and the port declined before ceasing operations in 1970.

When I visited in 2022 I was greeted by the silent grey flat emptiness of the Forth, its northern banks and once bustling stone quays abandoned in favour of factories and unkempt walkways. Across the river the southern bank comprising marshes and drab farmland stretched into the distance.

Half a kilometre back from the riverbank the house at 4 Mars Hill where the Thomsons lived still stands. A substantial Georgian house with enough room for the family and their servants to live in comfortably, it now backs onto a car park and has been taken over for use as an administration building by Alloa Council.

The Thomsons were a well-established family of merchants and shipowners. They also had interests in manufacturing, woollen and paper mills and coal mines. Their ships transported coal to the industrial centres of Britain and the Continent and timber between the Baltic Sea and Canada.[20]

Watson Thomson, John's father was born in Edinburgh and had moved to Alloa to be close to his business interests. His uncle, also a ship owner, had a successful business supplying Italian marble to the fine houses being built in the New Town of Edinburgh. Watson's cousins went on to set up the Ben Line Group which one hundred and fifty years later was Britain's largest offshore drilling contractor, employing over 2000 shore based and sea-going staff.[21]

Watson and his brother Andrew provided seed capital to their Edinburgh cousins but this was the limit of their involvement.

It was from the house in Alloa that John travelled to Greenock to board the *Nelson* in 1862. He sailed the twelve thousand miles alone to meet his older brother Andrew, my great-great-grandfather who was waiting for him in Port Chalmers. John's cousin Captain William Thomson, the first harbour master was also there.

Captain William Thomson (1822-1913) was the first Thomson to arrive in the new settlement. The 9th child in a family of twelve, his father, Andrew, died when he was seven years old. William attended school until the age of thirteen when he went to sea with his uncle, Captain Watson Thomson. William continued to serve on family ships and by the age of 21 had become a master mariner, commanding vessels trading in the Mediterranean, North America, the Philippines and Australia. In January 1852, he was in command of the *Moselle*, which took the first cargo of wool directly from Brisbane to England. Prior to this wool shipments had to be routed through Sydney.

---

20   Captain William Thomson. His Life, by Shirley Cameron. 2009.
21   Ben Line: Fleet List and Short History by Graeme Somner. World Ship Society. 1980.

TOP:
The Thomson Family Home, 4 Mars Hill, Alloa, Clackmannanshire, Scotland. (Photograph: R Fenwicke)

OPPOSITE TOP LEFT:
John's father, Captain Watson Thomson. (Portrait photograph courtesy of Dr Jane Batchelor)

OPPOSITE TOP RIGHT:
John's mother, Mrs Jane (Brown) Thomson. (Portrait photograph courtesy of Dr Jane Batchelor)

OPPOSITE BOTTOM LEFT:
Captain William Thomson: First Harbour Master, Otago Harbour & John's cousin. (Portrait photograph Courtesy: Toitū: Otago Early Settlers Museum.

OPPOSITE BOTTOM RIGHT:
Andrew Thomson (John's brother) and his wife, Jane Elizabeth (Dalgleish) Thomson. (Photograph courtesy of Blair Thomson.)

On a visit to Alloa, William sought and received agreement from the combined Thomson families to take two of their ships, the *Wanderer* and the *Signet,* and fit them out for the lucrative passenger trade the Australian gold rush had created. Both ships eventually arrived in Melbourne, where William went into business with two non-family members. He returned to Scotland to marry, but in his absence, the business, for whatever reason, foundered. He sailed back to Melbourne, taking with him his new wife, her cousins, one of his brothers, and his nephew, a thirteen-year-old Andrew Thomson, John's older brother. They arrived in Melbourne in November 1854 and settled in Geelong while William sold the ships and wound up the business. He was away on another voyage when his wife died, having lived in Australia for only four months.

In 1855, William met with the Hon. W. H. Reynolds who was in Victoria on behalf of the Otago Provincial Government scouting for new settlers to join the infant colony. Progress had been slow in getting the settlement established and after an initial flurry of new arrivals, ships had almost stopped calling because of the lack of harbour facilities. The total European population of the province was only 2400, (1350 males and 1050 females) - the population of Port Chalmers numbering 80 while those living in and around Dunedin, 700.

William, thirty-two, a widower, his business wound up, seized the opportunity to make a fresh start. Basing himself in Port Chalmers, he became the commander of the brig, *Thomas and Henry,* which was owned by the ubiquitous Mr Johnny Jones. This ship sailed between Otago and Sydney and/or Melbourne once every two to three months, bringing mail, news and goods to the small settlement.

Four years later, in 1859, Captain William Cargill, now the Superintendent of the Otago Provincial Council, asked William to become the first Otago Harbour Master. Having re-married, William, keen to spend more time at home, accepted. For the next twenty-three years he was to oversee the development of the upper (Dunedin) and lower (Port Chalmers) harbours as Otago grew quickly from a population of a few thousand to tens of thousands after gold was discovered in 1861. Andrew Thomson travelled with him to Port Chalmers, where he set up in business to prepare for the arrival in 1862 of his younger brother, John.

The discovery of gold in Central Otago in 1861 had transformed the small settlement. An observer (1862) reported his astonishment at seeing 'Port Chalmers crowded with shipping of every class from Dutch galliots to Black Ball liners of 2000 tons. The port itself was not impressive. The jetty was flimsily constructed of manuka posts and there were no warehouses for storing goods. The cargo was either directly discharged into hulks, of which there were two, or transferred directly to the Upper Harbour by means of lighters or small craft. At the Dunedin jetty, the boat could scarcely reach because of the state of the tide; there was a state of bustle and confusion not witnessed since leaving England, diggers in every variety of costume, with the dandy or "flash" man resplendent in scarlet shirt, white moleskin trousers, cabbage-tree hat with long black ribbons, and crimson silk scarf set off by a fringe of tassels dangling from the waist. To add variety, there were smart young clerks, customs-house officers, soldiers of the 70th in their bright scarlet tunics, policemen in blue with peaked leather hats, all set against a background of sailors and wharfingers. Such then was the old jetty in the summer of 1862.'[22]

John Thomson arrived into this chaos, expecting to join a successful business. His brother's investment in the goldfields however, meant

---

22   Ibid. McLintock.

he had no choice but to set off with Andrew into the wilds of Central Otago to re coup their finances. So starts the adventures recounted in *Voyages and Wandering in Far Off Seas and Lands,* which take him around New Zealand, the world and back again. In telling his story, he omits mention of his family and the day-to-day life involved in being an early settler in a new country. But we do get the full flavour of the man; his humour, his friendships and his search for meaning and understanding in himself and mankind.

The book is as he wrote it forty years after he set out for a new world. In his looking back at his time in New Zealand from his homes in Blairgowrie and Edinburgh in the early twentieth century, there are inevitably some minor errors of fact. These are corrected in the additional notes. I have also updated the spelling of Māori words and place-names, clarified some references and included others which add meaning to his story. I am certain John, who had marked passages for correction and updating in his personal copy of his book, would have approved.

The following material provides information regarding his life and his family in the thirty years between the end of 'Voyages' and John's death in Dunedin in 1933.

On November 24th, 1863, Andrew's and John's parents, Watson and Jane, arrived in Port Chalmers with their daughter Janet McFarlane, and her two sons, Falkland James and Norman. They arrived on the paddle steamer, *City of Dunedin*, captained by Janet's husband, James McFarlane. Built in Dunbarton for Mr Johnny Jones, the journey from Scotland to Port Chalmers had taken a very long 138 days. It was the custom then for Captains' wives to go to sea with their husbands. John's sister Janet was no exception and like the rest of her family was adventurous and well-travelled. Their first son, born on the ss

Falkland, was christened in Delhi, India. Alfred, their third child must have been relieved to be born two weeks after the family's arrival and not on the *City of Dunedin.*

By the end of that year, the McFarlane and the Watson Thomson families had set up house side by side, close to William Thomson's house at the top of Constitution Street, Port Chalmers. John's father lived there until he died at the age of 86 in October 1876. John's mother died two weeks after her husband and they are buried together in a plot in the Old Cemetery in Port Chalmers. In 1933, John was buried with them.

Andrew, John's god-fearing and upright older brother and business partner, married Jane Elizabeth Dalgleish in 1865 after she travelled out from Scotland. They had six children, three girls, and three boys. Jane died in 1884, at 39, Andrew marrying again in 1891, there being one son from this union.

Andrew was an active and contributing member of the early Port Chalmers community. He was an elder in the Presbyterian Church, a JP, a town councillor, and he served on many boards including the Otago Harbour Board, the local Licensing Trust and local school committees.

The business the brothers set up after their return from the goldfields in 1864, was diverse. Thomson Bros. operated from their premises in George Street as general merchants, ships' chandlers and agents, ironmongers, lighter agents, and importers and exporters. They also managed contracts for many public works. They owned and built ships, including the two schooners the *Bencleugh* and the *Friendship,* and were involved in both coastal and international trading. Andrew, with his family and community responsibilities, stayed in port while John, seeking adventure and unencumbered by a wife or children, travelled around New Zealand and the world conducting business on behalf of the firm, constantly seeking additional sources of revenue.

Newspaper reports from those years record Thomson Bros.' involvement in an enormous range of commercial ventures. Innovative and willing to the test new ideas and technology, they invested in schemes which were ahead of their time and thus not always successful. Andrew's strictness about the consumption and sale of alcohol did little to endear him to his more commercial contemporaries. The brothers were not unfamiliar with the courts, Andrew often seeking judgement for unpaid accounts or unfulfilled contracts. In April 1880, the police charged John with illegally storing 225 lbs of gunpowder (for the local quarry) on the premises in George Street. He had asked an employee to remove the bulk of the powder before the police arrived to document the infringement. Bail of £100 is recorded as paid, but no further information is available and I don't know if the proceedings went ahead.

In June 1884, after twenty years working side by side, the Thomson Bros. partnership was dissolved by mutual consent. Andrew had business ideas he wanted to explore and John, possibly inspired by his time on Macquarie Island, had inventions he wanted to develop.

Andrew took over the business as sole proprietor and continued to trade under the same name, Thomson Bros. His entrepreneurial spirit saw him become a founding owner and director of the Port Chalmers Gas Company. At the same time, he set up and ran a fish canning business and he also built and operated the first refrigeration plant in Port Chalmers, the second such plant in Otago. His business exported lamb carcasses and butter 'home' to Great Britain.

In 1892, after a series of business and financial setbacks, Andrew closed Thomson Bros. and sold the building on George Street. He later stood, (unsuccessfully) for parliament as a candidate for the Liberal Party in the Waikouaiti Constituency. He died in 1908 and is buried beside his first wife, Jane, in the Old Cemetery in Port Chalmers in the grave next to his parents and brother.

John Thomson left the partnership with £2000 and travelled to Melbourne, Australia, where he lived for the next decade. The following is a report in the New Zealand Times, dated the 23rd of July 1894, 'I ran across Mr J. S. Thompson, (sic) erstwhile of Thompson Bros., of Port Chalmers, the other day. He has been running about the country in the interests of his "Combined Air and Dasher Churn," the royalty rights of which he is anxious to dispose of for England and Europe. Like most inventors, he has kept his eye on every new thing in the same line, and has found nothing to excel his own invention. Mr Thompson has other ideas to patent at Home, but they are not in connection with dairy produce. Since he left Port Chalmers some eight years ago, Mr Thompson has lived in Melbourne, and in Victoria his churn has found many friends. But he does not intend to return to the Colony, and will most probably make the old Country his future home.'

John registered a patent in Queensland for an improved pneumatic butter churn in 1891. 'Thomson's Combined Air and Dasher Churn' went into production in 1893.

The Leader in Melbourne reported on the 23rd of January 1893, 'an illustration of an Australian invention patented by Mr J. S. Thomson of 52 Market Street, Melbourne. 'It has fallen to Mr Thomson to make the happy combination of the air and the dasher, securing the advantages of both systems without the evils of the other, and thus making on step onward in the advancement of scientific industry, and that a very important one.'

Throughout 1893, the Combined Air and Dasher Churn featured with illustrations in newspapers on the Eastern Australian seaboard. The Melbourne Weekly Times gave it a ringing endorsement on the

25th of February 1893. 'This invention, the Australian combination churn, hygienic, scientific, and up to date, deserves the support of Australians.' Modification of the churn meant it could also refine oil, scour wool and regulate the temperature and mix wine while it is being fermented.

There is no record of whether the churn ever became widely adopted for commercial use in Australia or whether John ever filed for a worldwide patent after his return 'home' to Great Britain some time in 1894.

In 1896, he married Margaret Anne Inches, the only child of Charles Hood Inches of Hope Park, Blairgowrie, in Perthshire. John was 52 and 'Maggie' was 45 when they married, so there were no children. An only child, Margaret had devoted her life to caring for her parents, who died in 1892 and 1893. For thirty years, she was also the Secretary of the Blairgowrie and Rattray Nursing Association and known for her independence and intelligence. Fittingly, Hope Park is no longer in private ownership and is now a home for the elderly. Maggie never visited New Zealand, but she met John's niece Jane, her husband Duncan Walker and their five children, including my grandmother, when the Walkers lived in Edinburgh in the first decade of the twentieth century.

The marriage certificate is the first official record we have of the addition of 'Sen' to John's name; the family believes he added Sen as a tribute to the Indian philosopher, Keshab Chandra Sen (1838—1884). John admired this man's teachings and likened Sen's quest for a single unifying belief system to beliefs expressed by Te Whiti o Rongamai, whose pacifist philosophy he never forgot. John's name was a work in progress because after the wedding he added Inches to his surname in honour of his wife's family.

The new couple divided their time between Hope Park in Blairgowrie, another home at 36 Royal Terrace in Edinburgh and travel around Great Britain.

However, John wasn't done with inventions and in 1897, he patented an apparatus for use by ships at sea to aid in navigation. Again, not much came of his work, but the machine was built, and one was donated to Blairgowrie High School in 1917. Designed to be used at sea, his invention served several purposes including recording all courses steered, as well as the relative position of vessels sighted, the colour of the lights showing and in the event of a collision, how both ships were handled and which, if either, was to blame. It had several other functions, but it is interesting to note, his concept predated the use of the 'black box' by sixty years.

John's inventions were never produced or used in any numbers. Perhaps they didn't work or he lacked the capital to take them to the next stage. Perhaps the writing and publication of his book was a distraction. We'll never know.

Voyages and Wanderings in Far Off Seas and Lands, published in 1912, was positively reviewed throughout the Empire. He was proud of it, regularly referring back to it throughout the rest of his life.

In 1919, Maggie died at their Edinburgh home aged sixty-eight. She is buried with her parents in the cemetery at Blairgowrie. Her will stipulated the income from her estate would go to John for the rest of his life on condition he would cease to be a beneficiary if he remarried. As John was a trustee of the will written in 1914, he had agreed to these conditions. He never re-married.

LEFT:
Margaret Inches Thomson :
(Photograph courtesy of Blair
Thomson)

BELOW:
Hope Park. Blairgowrie,
Perthshire, Scotland.
(Photograph: R Fenwicke)

TOP:
John Sen Inches Thomson with his great-great nieces and nephews, Dunedin 1931
(Publisher's father, Forrester, far right). (Photograph courtesy of Blair Thomson)

BOTTOM LEFT:
Margaret Inches Thomson (1851-1919) Gravestone: Buried with her parents, Blairgowrie, Scotland. (Photograph, R Fenwicke)

BOTTOM RIGHT:
John Sen Inches Thomson (1844-1933) Gravestone. Buried with his parents: Old Port Chalmers Cemetery. (Photograph, P Thomson)

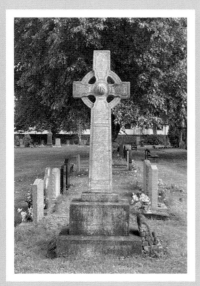

In the early 1920s, John returned to Otago and his family, living with Andrew's two unmarried daughters in Dunedin. My Uncle Graham recalled when he was four, being reprimanded by John for wearing a military-style jacket, indicating his pacifist views remained important throughout his life.

My father was eleven, when John Sen Inches Thomson, ship owner, businessman, gold miner, adventurer and explorer, inventor, philosopher and author, died in 1933, aged 88. His home at 780 George Street Dunedin is now a student flat. He left his estate to his nieces, not his nephews. He is buried with his parents in the old cemetery in Port Chalmers, no longer a stranger in the land he and his family now call home.

Rosy Fenwicke (Thomson)
Martinborough
New Zealand
1st May 2023.

VOYAGES and WANDERINGS in FAR-OFF SEAS and LANDS

PREFACE

IN PUBLISHING the following narrative of voyages and wanderings, I crave the indulgence of my readers. I can make no pretension to literary skill. Intended in the first instance for the interest and amusement of my friends, I have been encouraged to launch my craft upon a wide sea. Wherever it may go, I trust that its merits will be appreciated and its faults forgiven.

It is a true narrative of an old Colonial in one of the most distant frontiers of the Empire. My wanderings have been off the beaten track, and I believe they will be found in some respects unique, especially my early days in New Zealand and the life on the desert island in the Pacific.

Interspersed in the narrative will be found some thoughts which have influenced me amidst the rough and tumble of a chequered life, for there are times when the writings of the world's greatest teachers come home to one with especial emphasis and conviction. To a slight knowledge of the teaching of Goethe, Emerson, Ruskin and the Scriptures I myself owe much.

J. I. T. (1912).

CONTENTS

"Let me to-day do something that shall take
A little sadness from the world's vast store,
And may I be so favoured as to make
Of joy's too scanty sum, a little more."
Ella Wheeler Wilcox: 1902.

The Custom House Greenock, Scotland: Victorian Illustration.
The Keasbury-Gordon Photograph Archive. - Alamy.

CHAPTER I

DEPARTURE

JUST fifty years ago, (1862) the new A1 clipper ship *Nelson* lay at anchor at the tail of the bank off Greenock, the Blue Peter or salt beef flag flying at the foremast head, signifying that she was ready for sea, and about to sail.

The destination was Port Chalmers, New Zealand. Her officers and crew, as usual in the Patrick Henderson & Co. line were a capable and purpose-like lot, and in fairly good sea-going order, not more than half a dozen of them being "three sheets in the wind." This minority made the usual clatter and commotion, the result of loading up at the various Broomielaw[23] taps of the "fechtin', laughin', or greetin'" whisky.

The passengers, of whom there were several hundreds, were mostly young men, a few families, and several young women. They were drawn from nearly all ranks, though chiefly from the working-class, most of the districts of the Lowlands and the Highlands being well represented; on the whole a most respectable and promising

---

23   Main throughfare in Glasgow.

community, destined Empire-builders. Several have since risen in positions of power and eminence as merchants, squatters, inventors and one became a Supreme Court Judge of New Zealand.[24] As usual, there were one or two black sheep going abroad for the benefit of their friends at home!

Captain Brotchie, the much respected seaman's Chaplain, was a fine, jolly, pleasant old man, whose honest face commended his Christianity. He conducted a short service on deck, and gave good practical advice as to the conduct of life on board ship, and made an earnest appeal that "the best o' aw literature", the Bible, should not be neglected. After referring to the homes that the passengers were going to make abroad and the homes that they had left, the old Scotch paraphrase was sung, "O God of Bethel, by whose hand," by many quivering lips and with tearful eyes. Many of the ship's company sailing from the tail of the bank, and many now settled in all parts of the world affectionately remember occasions such as this.

The ship's bell rang to intimate that friends must leave for the shore: cruel and heart-rending in many an instance was the parting. All sorts of good wishes were exchanged once more; Mick entreated Patrick to be sure and write.

"I'll write ye ivery Saturday and drop it in the pillar box as we go along, sure."

"An' mind and sind us that nugget as big as a lump of coal."

"Yes, begorra, I will, if ye'll only come out and fetch it; so long, then, so long."

"Man the windlass," rings out from the Chief Officer. The command is re-echoed by the bosun's pipe and raucous tones, the

---

24   Sir John Edward Denniston (1845 – 1919). His brother G.L. Denniston became Provost of Dunedin.

hands tumble up on to the forecastle deck and turn to, and merrily the cable rattles through the hawse-pipe over the barrel of the windlass to the depths of the chain locker, whilst all the time the sailor's chanty is sung, more or less musically; it seemed to oil the machinery of the old-fashioned purchase, for in those days there were very few of the "patent" and the donkey-engine was almost unknown.

North and South and home again,
Round the world and all,
From Barry Dock to Callao,
From Limehouse to Bengal,
Where'er the old "Red Duster" flies,
Where'er a British hand's at work
You'd hear their chorus ring.

Refrain:
Oh it's "Frisco town for anchor up"
"Rio" for mains'l haul
As soldiers know their bugle notes
We know them one and all.
Leave her Johnny as we go,
"Missouri" or "Black Ball,"
Take your time from the chanty man
All Together ! Haul ![25]

The anchor's weighed, the sails are loosed, and set and trimmed to a light favouring breeze, and the good ship *Nelson* commences

---

25   J.K. Adkin

her career on a bright cloudless May morning, gradually leaving the familiar and very beautiful Clyde scenery.

We enter the Channel and begin to feel the heave of the Atlantic, and the land begins to sink in the distance and finally disappears, leaving our ship ––our little world –– a mere speck on the surface of the boundless ocean. On two occasions I have seen the Falls of Niagara, once in the summer time; mighty resistless power was the chief impression it left me then, and once in the winter, frozen over, when it seemed to tell of wild fantastic grandeur beyond description; but compared with the ocean, Niagara is a mere nothing. Covering five-sevenths of the entire surface of the globe, the ocean is inconceivable in its awful power. Full of an infinite variety of life, the inexorable destroyer of countless ships, human beings and even kingdoms; and yet, according to its mood, grand beautiful, calm, peaceful, joyous, aye, and angry and sorrowful too.

Looking down from the maintop gallant yard where I had gone in a spirit of bravado to assist in stowing the sail on a dark night in a heavy gale, the utter insignificance and feebleness of the little world beneath was duly impressed on me; the outline of what seemed like a shoe, or a very small boat, fringed with white froth, and away in the wake, a broad belt of phosphorescent light amidst mountainous seas, all seemed to tell of the might and the grandeur of the deep.

CHAPTER II

CROSSING THE LINE

FAVOURABLE winds carried us rapidly south into fine warm weather, and left us in the "doldrums," almost becalmed. "Ship-Ahoy," in a strange loud voice, as the shades of evening fell, startled the listless ship's company. "What ship's that?" − "Where from?" − "Where bound?" − "What cargo?" − "How many new candidates request permission to enter my dominions ?" − "Is whisky and ale still made in Scotland?" − "I will come on board at high noon tomorrow and will graciously accept a barrel of each, and will initiate the new subjects, provided they are all good men and true and approved of by my Executive" − "Au revoir," in a strong Aberdeen accent, ended the conversation, as Father Neptune took his departure in his burning sea-shell chariot, a half empty tar-barrel, which blazed away in our wake for hours afterwards.

Punctually at noon he put in a sudden and mysterious appearance over the bow, accompanied by Lady Neptune, seated on a gun-carriage, fitted up and highly decorated for the occasion, and drawn by six polar beers, all gorgeously caparisoned.

King Neptune presented a magnificent appearance; nearly seven feet high, he was adorned with richly-coloured garments of sea-weed, long white hair, and a beard reaching to his waist. He wore a large crown, and carried a three-pronged sceptre in his hand, which he used to poke in the ribs any unwary spectator, with the words, "Salute, you Scotch heathen."

A blast on his trumpet (a large conch-shell), and the procession moved along the deck. On the poop deck they were received by the captain, who provided refreshment and the bears exhibited a strange familiarity with, and no antipathy to, "Old Scotch."

Neptune now proceeded to deal with the "Greenhorns" among the sailors, who for the first time were crossing the line. Seated on a bunting-covered throne, on the roof of the house on deck, he was supported by his Royal partner, a doctor and a barber. A young apprentice was brought forward for examination. He was asked a few absurd questions, and the doctor felt his pulse, producing a large watch which looked uncommonly like a tin soup-plate with a painted clock-face. He shook his head solemnly, and declared that with the most approved scientific method he might pull through. He prescribed two pills, and ordered the patient to be well shaved, to arrest the high fever; this to be followed by gentle 'hydrophobic' treatment.

Shaving apparatus was produced, consisting of a large hoop-iron razor about a foot long in the blade, a bucketful of soft soap and whiting lather, a large-sized paint brush, and very large box of pills, which were quite the size of marbles, and composed of soap, grease and tar. The victim was well lathered, and every time he opened his mouth to answer the questions that were put to him, the brush was stuffed into it, the pills being administered at intervals.

They seemed to be rather difficult to swallow, and not particularly pleasant to taste.

The King next commanded that he should receive the 'hydrophobic' treatment, that he should be very gently dealt with, and afterwards be wrapped in warm cotton wool. At a wave of his trident the victim was ruthlessly seized and thrown head foremost into a huge bath, formed by a sail which had been suspended by the four corners and filled with salt water. To the accompaniment of fierce growls and yells he was mercilessly seized, ducked, shaken, and hugged, by the bears and almost drowned, and not till then was he allowed out, having successfully passed through his ever-to-be-remembered ordeal.

The process was repeated till all the hands that had not previously crossed the Equator had been treated.

The remainder of the day was spent in games, music, dancing and flirtation, the weather being very calm and hot, causing the pitch in the seams of the deck to boil. Some of the "greenhorn" passengers had the pleasure of sighting the line, by looking through a telescope, to the glass of which had been attached a narrow green riband.

CHAPTER III

LAND OH!

LEAVING the fiery tropics with the magnificent sunsets, sunrises, fierce rain and lightning storms, we picked up the south-east trade wind, and entered the cooler weather. The Northern Plough disappeared and the Southern Cross became visible. Off the Cape of Good Hope we experienced a heavy gale, with mountainous cross seas, which repeatedly broke on board, carrying away one of the life-boats, snapping the great iron davits like pipe-shanks, and sweeping the decks of everything moveable, giving one an object lesson of the mighty power of wind and sea combined.

It was hereabouts, but sixteen days sail from the nearest land that years afterwards, when making another voyage to New Zealand, the good ship *Dunfillan* caught fire. All hands were called and stationed, the steerage passengers were driven on deck by smoke, and the seat of the fire could not be found, though holes were bored into all compartments, and the mastheads examined for smoke. A noisy panic ensued, which finally settled into a grim silence interrupted occasionally by hysterical sobs from among the women. I had made up my mind that should necessity arise, rather than take to the boats, I would endeavour to persuade as many as possible to remain on the ship and alter the course to the Antarctic ice, distant about four days sail, and take our chances there, having the notion that what Esquimaux can do to sustain life, other determined white men could do also.

Fortunately the fire was discovered and extinguished. Then followed joy, more or less hysterical and noisy, thankful congratulations.

I have often thought that it is possible, even probable, that some of the "never-heard-of-more" ships, overtaken by some disaster in the Australian and New Zealand trade, may have reached the icy continent so near at hand, and that some of the exploring expeditions may yet come across long-lost survivors, and may also discover valuable fur-seal fields, which may be of real value to the human race.

In due time, the welcome cry of "Land Oh!" was heard, and we reached the coast of New Zealand without mishap. The nearest approach to an accident happened to myself; a heavy studding-sail boom was carried away, and fell from aloft on the spot where, a moment before, I had been seated. A second boom was sent aloft, which immediately smashed in the same way, and again fell in the same spot.

Life together on board ship brings out clearly individual character, whether good or bad, and society, as on shore, falls into sets or cliques. On the whole the Nelsonites got on together very pleasantly, although the Perthshire men maintained that Perthshire was the best shire in every way in Scotland. The Aberdonians replied "tak awa Aberdeen and 'twal mile roon aboot, an' fars Scotland"

and the Clydesiders that "there was nae place like doon the waater."

Slowly we sailed up along the east coast, passing the Snares, Stewart's(sic) Island and Waipapa Reef, where the s.s. *Tararua* was lost with 130 lives (1881), many bodies being buried on my brother-in-law's farm adjacent. I had sailed down the coast on the *Tararua* on the voyage previous to her disastrous shipwreck. I also sailed on the steamer *City of Dunedin* and the brigantine *Sea Serpent* on the voyages immediately preceding their disappearance with all hands. We then passed the Nuggets, Saddle Hill and Cape Saunders and finally reached the entrance of Otago Harbour, where lay on the south side the wreck of the steamer *Victory* and on the north the wreck of the *Genevere*. Purukanuie (sic)[26] and Murdering Beach[27],

26   Pūrākaunui Bay.
27   Called Whareakeake by Māori, Murdering Beach was the sight of conflict between Māori and early Europeans in December 1817, when the *Sophia*, a Hobart sealing ship carrying prospective settlers, anchored in Otago Harbour. Its captain James Kelly and a few others went to visit Whareakeake (then known to Europeans as "Small Bay") in an open boat. Among them was a settler named William Tucker who had built a house at Whareakeake two years previously, where he ran an export business in ornamental hei-tiki (pounamu neck pendants). At first they were welcomed, but when Tucker went into his house, the locals attacked Kelly, at the instigation of the chief Te Matahaere. In the ensuing melee three of the settlers were killed, including Tucker himself, who made it back to the boat but lingered in the surf begging his attackers not to hurt him before being "cut limb from limb". All the dead were eaten.
Kelly and the other survivors of the attack rowed back to the *Sophia*. He and his men then proceeded to kill large numbers of Māori, including a local chief named Korako. Their subsequent report claimed that the Māori had boarded the *Sophia* and were killed in the fight to retake it, and that Korako was captured and shot when he attempted to escape; historians caution that Kelly's account of events, made to justify the actions he took, exaggerates the danger he and his men were in. He went on to destroy multiple canoes and set fire to "the beautiful city of Otago". This probably refers to Ōtākou, on the other side of the harbour; however, the Whareakeake village does seem to have been burned at around the same time, and abandoned rather than rebuilt. A tapu was placed on the site and lifted in the 1860s.
The motive for the attack at Whareakeake is unclear. Kelly believed it was a

here visible, was the scene of the slaughter of some hundreds of Māoris (sic) of the olden times by the fierce Northern chief, Te Rauparaha, who with the newly introduced guns swept all before him, from one end of New Zealand to the other, killing thousands of his own countrymen. The following is from Bracken's Māori War Chant, Te Rauparaha fame song:[28] –

Moan the waves,
Moan the waves,
Moan the waves, winds and waters
Wafting the sad laments and wailings
Of the spirits that haunt the mountains,
Warrior souls, whose skeletons slumber.
Echoes of the craggy reeks,
Echoes of the rocky peaks
Echoes of the gloomy caves,
Echoes of the moaning waves,
Echoes of the gorges deep,
Echoes of the winds that sweep
O'er Pirongia's summit steep
Chant the Rangatira's praise,

---

reprisal for previous shootings of Māori by Europeans in the ongoing state of lawless conflict known as the Sealer's War. A later account accused Tucker of having stolen a Māori preserved head in 1811 and inaugurated the trade in these items; this is considered to be poorly evidenced. Local Māori tradition has it that the trouble arose over the *Sophia's* crew's treatment of the women at Ōtākou. Whareakeake was thereafter occupied by a succession of European households, and informally referred to as "Driver's Beach" or "Coleman's Beach" after two of them. However, on the first surveying map of the district (dated 1863) it was labelled "Murdering Beach". This remained its official designation until 1998, when the name Whareakeake was restored in the Ngāi Tahu Claims Settlement Act. https://en.wikipedia.org/wiki/Whareakeake.

28   "Musings in Maoriland": Thomas Bracken. The March of Te Rauparaha 1. https://nzetc.victoria.ac.nz/tm/scholarly/tei-BraMusi-t1-body-d2-d2.html

Chant it in a thousand lays,
Chant the Rangatira's fame,
Chant the Rangatira's name,
Te Rauparaha, Te Rauparaha.

Sound his praises far and near,
For his spirit still is here,
Flying through the gusty shocks,
When the sea ghosts climb the rocks,
Clad in foam shrouds, thick and pale,
Woven by the howling gale,
In the ocean's monster loom
Warp of green and weft of gloom,
Woven into sheets of white
By the wizards of the night;
Chant his name each ocean sprite,
Te Rauparaha, Te Rauparaha.

The Inis[29] came the hawk to kill,
Kapai! Rauparaha!
And yet the hawk is living still,
Kapai! Rauparaha!
The hawk can soar, the hawk can fight,
The Inis tried to stay his flight,
The hawk shall have a feast tonight,
Kapai! Rauparaha!

---

29   JIT. Inis should instead be, Tuis — a native bird of New Zealand.

Slaves should have but little words,
Kapai! Rauparaha!
Little songs for little birds,
Kapai! Rauparaha!
Little Inis should not try
With their little wings to fly
Where the hawk is perched on high,
Kapai! Rauparaha!

A pilot was soon alongside and on board, with my cousin, Captain William Thomson, the Chief Harbour Master for the Provinces of Otago and Southland. He gave me a very cordial welcome. Pilot Driver and he were amongst the earliest settlers in that part. My cousin had gone to sea as an apprentice with my father in the Atlantic trade. Dick Driver, as he was commonly known, deserted from an American whaler and took a Māori for his wife, by whom he had a much respected family. In appearance he was tall, spare, strong and fit and efficient in every fibre. He was the first pilot and one of the smartest; he used to beat square-rigged vessels over the bar and up to port, a distance of nine miles, which other pilots would not attempt to do, preferring to wait for a fair wind. He had had many strange experiences in the wild whaling days before European settlement.

CHAPTER IV

OTAGO

THE scenery about the lovely harbour of Otago is somewhat similar to that of the West Highlands of Scotland, but to an enthusiastic New Zealander it is much more beautiful

At the Māori kāik[30] are settled the remnant of what was at one time an important tribe. Here are still to be seen the tryworks erected by the whalers in the olden times for boiling their oil.

As we sailed up the harbour before a light, fair wind on a fine sunshiny day, the sails were clewed up and stowed, the anchor was let go, the chain cable thundered over the windlass and our voyage of 14,000 miles terminated. There landed in Dunedin from the *Nelson* the nucleus of many generations of sturdy settlers, and let us hope equal to, and superior to their worthy Pilgrim Fathers.

Port Chalmers, which is the Port of Dunedin, was at that time (1862) a small village of about 200 inhabitants. It nestles between two hills in Kopoti Bay[31], covered with lovely green bush, fern trees

---

30   Kāik, also kāinga and kāika: small settlement or village.
31   The locality was known to Maori as Kōpūtai. It where the Otago Block deed of

and heavy timber. Wooden houses were perched here and there, some others of "wattle and daub", and some of fern trees, and "the little church on the hill" occupied a prominent and picturesque position.

The view of the harbour, coast and islands formed a most enchanting picture. A few sailing craft lay at anchor in the roadstead, the brig *Thomas and Henry* being the most notable. In the early days of the settlement she was the mail packet, carrying supplies and the European mail from Sydney. The voyage was made once every six months under the command of Captain W. Thomson. The owner, Mr. J. Jones, one of the first white men to land in Otago, was the principal merchant, landowner, banker, and ship-owner, having been originally in the whaling trade. He had his own methods of settling disputed accounts with his captains, which although drastic, saved Court fees and lawyer's charges.

Inviting the unfortunate captain into his back yard, he proceeded to take off his coat, and then gave him such a thrashing, as to meet all demands of equity.

The arrival of the *Thomas and Henry* was a great event in those days — a cannon was fired, and this was the signal for a general holiday. The settlers mustered from far and near to receive much-needed supplies, and home-letters, and to discuss the latest intelligence brought by the mail, many of them attired in their simple and favourite grey or blue serge shirts, with broad collars of the same material.

Otago was originally a Free Church settlement and included

---

sale between local Ngāi Tahu and the New Zealand Company was signed in July 1844.

amongst the early arrivals was Captain Donald[32] Cargill, the first Superintendent of the province, who was a lineal descendent of Donald Cargill[33] of Blairgowrie, one of the martyrs burned at the stake. Doctor Burns, the pastor of the first Church was another of the first settlers; he was a nephew of the poet.

Although a religious community, a "lock-up" was necessary, but it was chiefly patronized by runaway sailors. Mr Monson, the jailer, used to let his prisoners out in the morning with the stern injunction to be sure to return by six o'clock at night, as otherwise they would be locked out!

Very primitive and simple were the early settlers. A well-known draper was offered for his corner section in Dunedin a large sum of money at the commencement of the gold rush, by one of the "New Iniquity," as the gold-seekers were called, the early settlers being denominated the "Old Identities." The offer was firmly refused, chiefly because Mr B. considered that the amount was more than the land was worth, and the would-be purchaser was told that he could not have come by his money honestly. Money was scarce amongst the community, and bartering was very common; a quarter acre section of land, which is now very valuable, was in those early days "swapped" for a cart-wheel!

---

32   JIT changed this to, Captain William Cargill, in the margins of his personal copy of Voyages and Wanderings.

33   Donald Cargill (1619-1681) was born in Rattray and was a Presbyterian minister and Covenanter. The Covenanters pledged to maintain their own way of worship following the signing of the National Covenant in 1638. But during the latter half of Charles II's reign, Presbyterianism was outlawed by the Scottish Parliament. Ministers who resisted were evicted from the Church. Cargill, like many other ministers, was forced to hold illegal meetings called 'conventicles'. He was eventually captured in 1681 and taken to Edinburgh where he was found guilty of treason and hanged. https://www.snowroads.com/history/places/cargill-s-leap

CHAPTER V

THE GOLDFIELDS

It was shortly after the first gold discoveries that I landed. Gabriel Read[34] had arrived in Dunedin with a large quantity of gold, and the Gabriel's Gully goldfield named after him as the discoverer, was the scene of the greatest excitement and bustle. Hartley and Ryley[35] then arrived with pack horses, laden with sacks, made chiefly of moleskin trousers, containing eighty-seven pounds weight of gold, having discovered the Dunstan and Molineux(sic)[36] river district.

The whole community caught the gold fever; ordinary occupations

---

34   On 23 May 1861, in the gully which still bears his name, Read discovered gold, 'shining like the stars in Orion on a dark frosty night.' It was this discovery which revealed the potential of gold in Otago, and thereby initiated the series of discoveries and rushes which were to transform the economic, social and political life of the province. https://teara.govt.nz/en/biographies/1r3/read-thomas-gabriel

35   Horatio Hartley and Christopher Reilly; Californian veteran gold prospectors.

36   Māori called this river Mata-au (meaning surface current) or Waimatau; Captain Cook called it the Molyneux after his sailing master; the Lay Association under whose auspices Otago was settled by members of the Free Church of Scotland in association with the New Zealand Company decided to call it the Clutha, being the Gaelic for Glasgow's great river Clyde. Contributions to the Early History of New Zealand (Otago): Dr Hocken. Pub: Sampson Low &Co. 1898.

were abandoned, and everyone that could be spared, men, boys, and some women also, started for the goldfields. In those days there were no roads to speak of, and only a few tracks, as much of the country was unexplored; few horses were available, so that most folk had to travel on foot, carrying their own tents, blankets, tools and provisions, forty to sixty pounds weight being reckoned an ordinary swag.

On landing I expected to find myself the junior partner of a fairly prosperous business, but riches had taken wing, and all that was left of the business was invested in the goldfields and in mining property. And so it happened that ere long I found myself amongst the "rushers," tramping, but without a swag and in company with my brother Andrew. He had come out two years previously for the second time. We had youth, health, strength, and stout hearts, and determined to retrieve our losses. So we trudged manfully through mud and creeks, in all kinds of weather, doing occasionally, over thirty miles a day.

We held shares in the Weatherstone water race[37] [38]. The company

---

37   The first joint-stock mining company registered in Otago bought the water race and sluicing works of the Weatherstone Water Company. Diggers, Hatters and Whores: The Story of the New Zealand Gold Rushes, by Steven Eldred-Grigg. Random House New Zealand, 2011.

38   The "Weatherstone Water Company" (was) the first mining company registered in Otago, and probably in New Zealand, under the provisions of " The Joint Stock Companies Act, 1860". The capital was fixed at £5,000, in 1000 shares of £5 each. It was started in 1862 as a private company and has been most successfully worked ever since the sum of £11,000 having during that time been realised for water. The present race drains an area of 20,000 acres and is constructed for four miles along the highest ranges around Weatherstones crossing the top of the saddle range, opposite the Blue Spur, Gabriel's, to which a branch race could be out at any time, if desirable, at a small cost. It is from this reservoir and race that the town of Lawrence now derives its water supply. Early Gold Discoveries in Otago by Vincent Pyke. M.H.R. Otago Daily Times and Witness Newspapers Company, Ltd. 1887.

had built a reservoir, pretty much annexing all water rights of the districts, for there were practically no mining laws in those days. We dug a ditch or race along the hillsides for some miles, which carried the water to the heights of the goldfield. The water was gladly purchased by the miners, for water is an essential to them in their work. The company, while charging for the water, reserved to themselves the option of putting one of their shareholders, who were all working miners, into each of the eight best claims on the field, these receiving each a man's share of the gold at the wash-up.

This proved to be a good venture, financially and was the means of a fresh start. The claim allotted to me was held by a party of Manxmen, runaway sailors, strong, hearty, jovial fellows, rejoicing in being their own masters and in having "struck it rich!"

Jim Addy a Blue Nose[39] from New Brunswick, was also of the party. Jim took a kindly interest in me. I was a "tenderfoot" or "new chum," only seventeen years old. He initiated me in the art of cooking chops, baking damper, sluicing, cradling, panning off, etc. Jim was rough and careless in outward appearance but he had a heart of gold. He had followed the diggings in various parts of the world and had some strange experiences. His soft slouch hat had been pierced by a pick in the hands of a murderous mate, when working underground. It was given out to be an accident with no worse result than a split head but Addy always believed his mate intended to kill him, and rob him of his share of the gold.

Alas! He had a tragic end after all, when working on the wild Kawara(sic)[40] River, the principal branch of the Molyneux. A heavy flood, caused by the bursting away of a hillside, which had slipped

---

39   Blue Nose: a person who advocates a rigorous moral code
40   Kawarau River

into the river and dammed back an enormous accumulation of water, came down in the night time, carrying disaster and death to the miners camped on its banks. Addy, his mate Gascoigne, their tent and twelve pounds weight of gold, which was buried in the floor were swept away. Addy was drowned but Gascoigne managed to reach the shore a long distance down, barely alive.

My claim was a surface one, and I found the work for the first week or so very hard, but later got quite accustomed to it. The richest ground was close to the reef, in old water-worn channels. Such a lead or gutter crossed our claim, in which we would often see the gold sparkling, and from which we could occasionally wash a quarter of an ounce in one tin dish. This gutter was finally run out on the surface, so that in pulling up the grass tussocks, we found the gold sparkling and adhering to the roots.

The gold-mining and gold-saving appliances were crude and wasteful as compared with those of modern times. The Tuapeka goldfields were mostly surrounded by hills, Gabriel's Gully being a long, deep valley of several miles in length. Tents were perched in every possible situation. Scattered over were small roughly-made wooden windlasses. Round the mouths of shafts were great heaps of blue and yellow soil like huge molehills. Cradles, sluice boxes, tubs, puddling machines, and streams of muddy water completed the landscape.

The place has now been altered beyond recognition. Huge chasms have been dug, right down to the reef, to the roots of the mountains, and the mountains themselves literally removed, having been sluiced down the valley, by means of enormous hydraulic operations.

A larger tent than the average, with here and there a flag flying, generally British or American, would indicate a store, where all the necessaries could be purchased, or exchanged for gold dust.

Streams of new chums kept pouring down the hill-track. They had to stand the chaffing and running-fire of the diggers, and cries such as, "Jo, Jo, Jo," "Who's your hatter?" "What price gaiters?" "What price quill driving?" "Lime-juicer," etc., according to "the cut of the jib," or other new-chummish peculiarity that might be noticeable, and always accompanied with boisterous good humour.

My first attempt at cooking a plum-pudding was rather startling. After boiling the conglomeration in a galvanized bucket, and pouring off the hot water, what was my surprise to find quite a quantity of gold in the bottom of the bucket! What the connection was between the gold and plum-pudding passed my comprehension. My mates, on noticing my surprise, laughed heartily, and insisted that if the pudding was rightly made that was what always happened in gold country.

The explanation was that the bucket has been used for carrying rich wash-stuff on the claim to the panning-off tub, the heavy gold had worked into the folded seams of the bucket and the boiling water had simply boiled it out.

"Rushes," or general stampedes, were breaking out in various directions: the "Blue Mountain Rush" was memorable as being a "rank duffer." A miner arrived at the township with a quantity of gold and reported that he had "struck a patch." Hundreds of miners accompanied him away over the trackless mountains, but either he could not find the locality or he had lied. The angry miners purposed to lynch him on the spot, and he narrowly escaped, partly through my brother's influence, from having his ears cut off.

The diggers generally were a lawless set, but dispensed amongst themselves a rough justice which was a terror to evil-doers.

Some were Californian diggers with memories of the Vigilance Committee[41], old lags, convicts, and Chinamen. Many trades and professions were represented, and there were gentlemen's sons and an occasional titled party, who by stress of circumstances was obliged though not ashamed to handle the pick and shovel. Some convict bush-rangers from Australia were amongst them. They stuck up the Mangatuie(sic) Road[42] one day and every passer-by was taken away into the bush, tied up and robbed. We had dispatched a trusty messenger with sufficient money to buy a pair of horses. He was the only man to escape that day, having looked in at the bushrangers' tent, and rested a while at their fire while they were engaged in tying up others less fortunate in the bush.

One of these bushrangers, Garret[43], an old Australian convict, I saw repeatedly afterwards. Another famous bushranger was

---

41 "Whereas it has become apparent to the citizens of San Francisco, that there is no security for life and property, either under the regulations of society as it at present exists, or under the law as now administered; Therefore the citizens, whose names are hereunto attached, do unit themselves into an association for the maintenance of the peace and good order of society, and the preservation of the lives and property of the citizens of San Francisco, and do bind ourselves, each unto the other, to do and perform every lawful act for the maintenance of law and order, and to sustain the laws when faithfully and properly administered; but we are determined that no thief, burglar, incendiary or assassin, shall escape punishment, either by the quibbles of the law, the insecurity of prisons. the carelessness or corruption of the police, or a laxity of those who pretend to administer justice." Virtual Museum of the City of San Francisco.

42 Mangatuie Road is Maungatua Road -- the main road to the gold fields from Dunedin in the late nineteenth century.

43 Garrett arrived in Dunedin on the *Kembla* on 7 October 1861 en route for the Otago goldfields. Garrett and several companions carried out highway robbery of fifteen men, they stole gold and property worth some £400 at the foot of the Maungatua range, on the track between Gabriel's Gully and Dunedin. He fled to Sydney where he was arrested in December, sent back to Dunedin and sentenced to eight years goal in May 1862. https://en.wikipedia.org/wiki/Henry_Beresford_Garrett

"Captain Moonlight,"[44] the most remarkable criminal of that time who was executed in Sydney. He was originally the Rev. Andrew George Scott, the Church of England clergyman on the Egerton goldfield.

One of the principal gold "rushes" was the Dunstan Rush, on the Molyneux river; the whole mining community with very few exceptions, were infected by the fever, and started for the El Dorado, abandoning claims, shanties, mining machinery, even articles of clothing, all except the absolute necessaries. Except swagging, packing on horseback was the only means of conveyance, and freight was carried at two shillings a pound by the fortunate few who possessed horses. We had room to spare on our horse, and were paid five pounds for carrying a fifty pound sack of flour for a distance of forty miles. As the men got fatigued by the length of the journey and their heavy swags they often threw away all but the absolutely indispensable.

The journey lay over trackless hills, in parts destitute of firewood, which we had sometimes to carry in addition for several miles in order to "boil the billy,' but the native tussocky grass was often used instead.

The Molineux is a wild, rapid river, flowing for the most part in a deep narrow channel, which it has worn for itself in the course

---

44   Scott was born in Ireland, the son a clergyman. The family moved to New Zealand in 1861, with Scott intending to try his luck in the Otago goldfields. However, the Māori Wars intervened and Scott signed up as an officer and was wounded at the battle of Ōrākau Pa. He left New Zealand in 1868 without ever visiting the goldfields, and was appointed lay reader in Victoria with the intention of entering the Anglican priesthood on the completion of his service. He was then sent to the gold mining town of Mount Egerton where he started his career in crime, serving multiple prison terms. He was convicted of shooting a police officer in a fire fight and executed by hanging in 1880. https://en.wikipedia.org/wiki/Captain_Moonlite

of the ages. It drains a large watershed, and the cold lakes and is subject to heavy floods. Its waters are singularly cold, having come from the snow and glaciers of the high mountains. The number of fatal accidents that have occurred on this most dangerous river is almost incredible.

Having left the Hungry Ranges, New-Chum Point, Manuherikia Junction, Mutton Township (the diggers are never at a loss for nomenclature), we arrived at the Gorge on the Molineux, now named Clyde. The scene presented was most lively. The town was mostly canvas, and was at first called Canvastown. Here and there was a general store or gold-buying agency, with dry stone walls, flags of different nationalities, numbers of pack horses and great crowds of diggers. Many came in to sell their gold and purchase stores and many to have a good (!) spree, and knock down their hard-earned money.

Grog shanties were in abundance and grog was cheaper than provisions. Flour was 2s. 6d. per pound, tea 6s. and everything else in proportion.

A teamster arrived with a load of flour, and insisted on 2s. 6d. a pound for all of it. He would not accept 2s., so the diggers just helped themselves and gave him nothing; his avarice exceeded his prudence and a fair profit.

Our road to the Dunstan lay through a variety of fine scenery, but chiefly the rolling plains and hills covered with native grass, suitable for sheep farming. Rabbits had just been introduced, and the sportsman who first landed them received great credit and praise for his enterprise. But the farmers very soon changed their tune, when they found the rabbits multiplied so tremendously, that instead of land feeding four or five sheep per acre, four or five acres per sheep were necessary. In some districts the rabbits have become such a pest as to eat up even the grass roots, leaving nothing but black soil. As a result, for a time the value of station property was depreciated by millions of pounds.

Our party was one of the first to ascent the Kawara river, the principal branch of the Molineux, and we struck a fairly good claim. The method of working the beach claims then in vogue was by building dams as far out into the river as possible, baling out the water from the enclosed space by means of buckets, spear, or Californian pumps, and then putting the payable wash dirt through the cradle, or sluice-box.

> *The wash through the sluice-box sailing slow,*
> *And the heaps of tailings high,*
> *The gold shines in lucid lines*
> *As the dirt goes drifting by,*
> *Peeping from out the crevices small*
> *Of the ripples with gorgeous glare,*
> *Yellow and bright does it meet the sight,*
> *Shining, rough and rare.*[45]

A cradle resembles a baby's cradle in shape and is rocked by hand in a somewhat similar fashion. The gold-bearing soil is shovelled on to the perforated hopped plate on top, on which water is continually poured. This has the effect, together with the rocking motion, of completely disintegrating the mass, the rough stones roll off the hopper plate, and the remainder falls through on to a series of sloping shelves beneath, provided with ripples or other

---

45   T. McMahone.

obstructions, which cause the heavy gold to become fixed in the crevices. The last shelf of all is covered with a piece of plush or woollen blanket, and sometimes a copper plate is used at the tail, covered with quicksilver. The quicksilver amalgamates the fine gold, and is afterwards evaporated by the application of heat to the amalgam, leaving behind the pure gold, worth about £4 per ounce.

Gold-mining has great attractions for sanguine people especially, and many men seem unable to resist the temptation to "rush." I remember one such, who had been on the principal goldfields of the world, lifting up his hands to heaven, and solemnly swearing that he would not go to another rush, not if it was only over the first range of hills, and though the gold was a foot thick; and I heard that shortly afterwards he was again infected by the gold microbe, and had started for the new field.

> *The swags to our back for the wild bush tracks,*
> *Say "Come" and we now must go*
> *To the endless trees and the free fresh breeze,*
> *Where the pines and the nikans grow,*
> *The pick, the shovel and the dish once more,*
> *The camp and the manuka bed,*
> *The tent and the fly, and the mopok's cry*
> *At night in the trees o'erhead.* [46]

Gold-mining as a rule is not profitable; every ounce of gold is said to cost more than it sells for, and there are many more unlucky diggers than lucky ones. The follies and extravagance of some lucky one have occasionally been very extraordinary, as for instance,

46   Unattributed.

hiring a hotel or grog shanty for days together and supplying free drinks to all comers. One miner was known to put a bank-note between two slices of bread and butter and give the sandwich to his dog to eat. Horseshoes were made of solid gold and a horse was shod with them. This happened in Victoria on the occasion of an election. Only a few "strike it rich," as for instance the finders of the Bendigo nugget, "Welcome Stranger," weighing 190 pounds and worth about £9000, and the Wahi[47] (sic) mine-owners who have taken out £9,000,000 sterling in gold altogether.

---

47   Waihi

CHAPTER VI

RETURN TO THE COAST

My brother and I ultimately determined to abandon the goldfields, and to return to civilization. We were not sorry to forsake the eternal mutton and damper; damper is simply flour and water made into a dough, which is covered with hot wood ashes in the fireplace at night, and is found thoroughly cooked in the morning. The rough tent life and plain fare had, however, agreed with us. Constitutionally strong and hearty, we had to admit that the "simple life" had scored.

On our first day's journey towards Tuapeka, we had to contend against a snowy blizzard in our faces the most part of the way. We nearly lost our faithful dog "Tiger" crossing the Manuherikia river. He was a strong, heavily-built animal, and, like most diggers' dogs carried the tent, strapped pack-saddle fashion, across his back. We had forgotten about him on entering the boat, and only at mid-stream did we notice him attempting to follow us swimming, he had been carried by the fierce current a long way down the river, being hampered by his heavy load. However we managed to pick him up, and were very pleased to find that after a short time he was little the worse.

The second day the weather was somewhat better, but the snow was deep in places and the track obliterated, and how my brother and "Tiger" together were able to pick up the right spurs and leading ranges was a mystery to me.

When camping the night previously under the lee of a big rock, our supply of mutton chops for the next day's journey had, as we thought, been securely placed out of reach. In the morning we discovered that "Tiger" had disposed of the lot! Tea and damper with nothing "tilt" made a bad early breakfast, and it was two o'clock before we reached the nearest supplies. I was completely exhausted *en route,* and would have given anything to be allowed to sleep for a short time in the snow, but Andrew was inexorable, and by dint of an occasional thoroughly good shaking, would set me on my feet and start me going again.

At last we reached Gairdner's sheep station, and made the acquaintance of Mr Robert Gairdner, who became a life-long friend. He was a kindly, genial soul, who sacrificed himself for the welfare of others.

At the station were camped a large number of diggers from Australia, held up by the storm. The first place we looked in at was a large frame tent, in which were about forty men, mostly asleep on the ground, and lying very close together, the only standing place being a narrow passage up the centre.

"Tiger" took up a position about the centre. Having just come through the creek he was, like ourselves, soaking wet, and he started to shake himself. Oh the yells, roars, curses, boots, and anything and everything portable, that were levelled at poor "Tiger!" I think I hear and see it all yet. It was a sudden awakening. We considered it only discretion promptly to withdraw, but we heard hearty laughter shortly afterwards, and concluded that "Tiger's" shaking had been a relief from the tedium of waiting.

We crossed the river in a bullock-hide boat. I have been in Māori and American Indian canoes, but this was the most "cranky" of any, and it did not have the bearings even of a coracle. Our orders from the Commander were to shed our hair in the centre, in case of a capsize, sit perfectly still, pay half-a-crown each, and look pleasant.

The ingenuity of the digger, many of them being handy men from the sea, is amazing. Another appliance that we met with on that trip, for crossing rivers, was a boatswain's chair, attached to a rough home-made block, running on a hand-made rope of rough New Zealand wild flax, identical in principle to a coastguards, life-saving apparatus.

Our run down the "Devil's back-bone" was rapid, and as is usual where his majesty is concerned, was a case of *facilis descensus*. We joined hands, slid, staggered, tobogganed (minus the toboggan), like boys out of school, and arrived safely in the valley below, where there was no snow. The sun was shining bright, and a big log fire, which had just been left by some waggoners with their teams, was blazing.

We had a good meal, got thoroughly dried and rested, and made a fresh start. The flooded creek was the first obstacle. Andrew walked straight through it. My knee-boots were leaky and I wished to keep as comfortable as possible, so I made a run and a big jump at the narrowest part and where the current ran strongest. I landed on the far side in stiff clay, in which my heels remained fast, and not having weight enough to carry me over the centre, as an engineer would express it, I slowly fell back into the stream, and was swept down by the rapid current, but finally effected a landing. My brother considered it highly amusing, and laughed heartily. I didn't, and stood wondering whether to go back to the fire and get dried again or not, but decided to go on as I was, and we reached Weatherston's after dark, having to feel our way amongst shafts, ditches and all kinds of obstacles. It was a rough life, but we had learned the wisdom of adapting ourselves to our surroundings, and with robust health and sound sleep, our troubles sat lightly.

We finally reached Dunedin, after six months on the goldfields, and were surprised to observe the wonderful progress the town had made in every direction during that time.

It was many years before we again touched mining property. The banks of the golden Molineux had been wrought from end to end, and as far into the river as possible; the bed of the river was supposed by sanguine individuals to be "paved with gold." A few crude dredges of various kinds, worked by hand and by paddle wheel, driven by the force of the current, were in operation, some of them being very successful. Our twin screw steamer *Jane*, of which Mr Wilson, of Earlstoke owned one-third, was dispatched to the Molineux, and there fitted up with a twenty-six bucket dredging plant, which was operated by her own steam power. It was then found that steam power dredge-mining could be worked effectively and cheaply.

This was the *first time* in the world's history on which steam dredging was worked in gold-mining. Although we cannot lay claim to be the first to originate the new method, we were the first to be in actual working. [48],[49],[50]

48   8 April 1881: Clutha Leader: "The inhabitants of Balclutha were a little surprised
        on Wednesday evening by noticing a steamer steaming up the Kauo(sic) branch
        of the river. She turned out to be the *ss Jane* from Dunedin, our old friend
        Captain Gordon M'Kinnon being in charge. The Jane is owned by Messrs
        Thomson Bros, Port Chalmers, who have entered into a dredging speculation
        at the six mile beach, ten or twelve miles above Tuapeka mouth. The Jane has
        all the necessary machinery on board and will, on her arrival at the six mile
        beach, be fitted up and set to work as a dredge for gold. She left Port Chalmers
        on Tuesday morning at 4 o'clock, and arrived at Coal Point at 11 p.m. where she
        anchored for the night. On Wednesday morning at 7 o'clock she entered the river,
        finding 11 feet in the new channel, and proceeded to Kaitangata for coal. She
        then returned to the mouth, took the cross channel at the bottom of the island and
        came up by the Kaou branch. The shallowest water found throughout the route
        was 5 feet, the Jane drawing 4 feet 10 inches. Captain M'Kinnon says he never
        found the channel in better order. The Jane was moored at the bridge, here, all
        Wednesday night, and resumed her voyage yesterday afternoon. We hope the
        Captain will have the same experience of the channel up river as he has had so
        far. We may add that Mr Tyson is on board and will be in charge of the dredging
        operations.

49   15 April 1881: Otago Daily Times: The arrangements for conducting dredging
        operations along the beaches of the Molyneux by Messrs Thomson Bros., of Port
        Chalmers, are proceeding apace (says the Tuapeka Times). A small twin-screw
        steamer (18 h.p.) named the *ss Jane*, which will be fitted up and set to work as
        a dredge, arrived at Tuapeka Mouth last Sunday, conveying a large quantity of
        the machinery necessary for the prosecution of operations. The remainder of
        the plant will come by rail to Lawrence, and thence be conveyed by wagon to
        the spot where the steamer is at present launched. It is expected that dredging
        will be commenced in about six weeks from date. The steamer is now lying in
        the river - about two miles above Tuapeka Mouth. In the course of a few weeks
        she will travel up the stream to a place known as the Six-mile Beach-about
        midway between Tuapeka Mouth and the Beaumont Ferry. Mr John Tyson, who
        is well known and widely respected in this and other parts of New Zealand, is in
        charge of the dredge. The services of a better or more trustworthy man could not
        possibly have been secured by the Messrs Thomson.

50   "A small spoon dredge worked one stream as early as 1863, and as the years went
        by the awkward craft grew bigger until they became a way of trawling gold that
        worked only when backed by a thumping weight of money. Franz Siedeberg and
        Hermann Schultz, goldfields traders, strove to better the spoon dredge and later
        the current-wheel dredge. Dredges of the latter type floated on pontoons and
        were worked by paddle-wheels. The first may have been launched in 1864 on the
        Manuherikia, but far better was the machine designed and floated four years later

Shortly afterwards there was a great boom in steam dredges throughout New Zealand and Australia, and fortunes were quickly made by some. The method is now in general use in all gold-bearing countries, even in Siberia, Alaska and the Philippines.

Unfortunately on account of her draught, the steamer could not be taken up the river much beyond Tuapeka, where the ground was poor. The difficulties were very great, as the Molineux is in many places very rapid and wild, but with engines going at their highest pressure, with sometimes two hundred fathoms of hauling lines out ahead, block and tackle purchase, and hand winches, it was successfully negotiated without accident. [51]

The return journey down the river was made in about as many hours as it had taken days to ascend. It was a most enjoyable and thrilling experience, steering through the rapids, and amongst rocks, shoals, and snags, and out over the bar, the mouth of the river having just lately shifted more than a mile away, and there was nothing to mark the new channel.

I got enough gold out of the pioneering enterprise to make marriage rings and a brooch for my good wife. [52]

---

by Siedeberg. 'Current-wheelers' were soon working the fields widely." Diggers, Hatters and Whores. The Story of New Zealand Gold Rushes by Steven Eldred-Grigg. Random House, New Zealand. 2011.

51 In 1887, Choie Sew Hoy took up claims in the lower Shotover River and worked them with a newly built steam-powered bucket-ladder dredge. It was an immediate success. https://teara.govt.nz/en/artwork/8628/choie-sew-hoys-dredge.

52 12 September 1883, Southland Times, Bluff Harbour Board: A letter from Messrs Thomson Bros. offered the screw steamer Jane with dredge attached for sale or hire. Consideration adjourned till next meeting.

CHAPTER VII

SHIP *PARISIAN* AND THE CHATHAM ISLANDS

OUR first investment in floating property was the ship *Parisian,* a beautiful model of a ship and a fast sailer (sic), but we soon discovered that it had a great many "dummy" bolts, that is, instead of long copper bolt fastenings, four to six feet in length, clinched outside and inside, mere bold heads had been substituted. So the ship wanted fastening. It worked in a sea-way like a basket, and consequently leaked considerably.

In the absence of graving docks, it was necessary to have the ship "hove down", a method adopted by Captain Cook when on his visit to New Zealand[53], but seldom or never used nowadays. The process was as follows: Two coal hulks were moored on one side of the ship, heavy block and tackle purchases were made fast to the lower mast heads of the ship and to powerful winches on board the hulks. By heaving down on the winches, the mast heads of the ship were hove down to the decks of the hulks, and the whole of the broadside of the ship and keel exposed, and made get-at-able for repairs. After one

---

53   It is unlikely Captain Cook used this method.

side had been repaired and coppered the ropes were slacked up, the hulks shifted to the other side, and the process repeated.

She made a voyage to Vancouver Island carrying diggers to the Frazer River goldfields, and returned with a load of Oregon timber. On a voyage to London, she came into collision with another ship in the English Channel and considerable damage to both ships resulted. A third trip was to Abyssinia with Government stores for the war.[54] Here she lay a long while on demurrage, and finally carried most of her cargo back to Bombay.

Wars bring tremendous evils in their train, and one of them is the discovery by merchants and contractors that "war is good for business," and so it happens that wars are promoted by businessmen whilst the ignorant multitude are shouting, "patriotism," "justice," "revenge," etc. There is every reason to believe that one of the chief causes of the Russo-Japanese war was that timber syndicate, in which the wealthiest in Europe were participants, coveted and sought to possess hugely valuable timber rights, and had influence enough to obtain the assistance of the Russian military.

What a stupendous mockery of civilization, peace and Christianity, are our battleships and armies, with all their tremendous cost and misdirected energy, which if reasonably directed, might extinguish poverty and want throughout the kingdom, and bring health, strength and happiness to tens of thousands, together with a large measure of honesty and consideration for others, for a vast deal of the thieving at present is the direct result of desperate want.

There are ninety and nine that work and die
In want and hunger and cold,

54   Abyssinia, modern day Ethiopia: Anglo-Abyssian war 1867-1868.

That one may revel in luxury
And be lapped in the silken fold!
The ninety and nine in their hovels bare,
And one in a palace of riches rare.

From the sweat of their brow the desert blooms,
And the forest before them falls;
Their labour has builded humble homes
And cities with lofty halls
And the one owns the cities and houses and lands
While the ninety and nine have empty hands.[55]

My next voyage was to the Chatham Islands in our small ketch *Redcliff* on a trading expedition. This was the first command of our young skipper, and I soon found that he could take the sun, and find his latitude but that longitude reckoning was quite beyond his powers. The group of islands are only thirty-eight by twenty-five miles in extent, so the risk of missing them was considerable. Fortunately we had a steady fair wind, which increased latterly to a gale, and we made excellent landfall and anchored in Waitangi Bay on the fifth day out.

Although so near to New Zealand, only 536 miles distant, the communications with the outside world from Chatham Islands at that time was only once every six months. So our arrival was very welcome, and the settlers clamoured to receive their letters. I brought news of the capture of Paris by the Germans (1871), which caused much astonishment, and made them eager for further news of what was happening abroad.

---

55   Rose E. Smith: First two verses of three verse hymn- music by David
         Sankey.1874.

We sailed round the islands to the various boat harbours, loading wool, hides, etc., and narrowly escaped shipwreck, having to beat the vessel through three lines of breakers, but with no further mishap than the loss of a dinghy.

The natives of the islands are called Māorioris (sic)[56]. They are a different race from the Māoris of New Zealand, being of a smaller build, with features somewhat Jewish. They were numerous at one time, but the Māoris came over from New Zealand in their war canoes and killed off most of the tribe.[57]

The main road across the principal island lies through a singular brackish lake, several miles in diameter. It takes the horses well up to the girths, but it is quite safe, except in fogs, when one is in danger of being lost. Occasionally the sand-spit between the ocean and the lake is broken away by the action of the sea. The eels, many of which are a great size, by some curious instinct become aware of it, and make a great rush for the sea in such enormous numbers that the shallow banks get covered with them. They are easily killed by hitting them with sticks. Sea birds congregate in great numbers to feast on them, and the spectacle is altogether most extraordinary.

The Chathams used to be much frequented by American whalers, and a number of the beaches are strewn with wrecks. Pitt's Island I found inhabited by four generations of the name of Hunt. The arrival there of a vessel is a time of great rejoicing, and very hearty hospitality is offered. On these occasions it is said that the

---

56   Moriori.

57   In November 1835 about 900 people of the Ngāti Mutunga and Ngāti Tama tribes migrated to the Chatham Islands on the ship *Lord Rodney*. Initially welcomed by the Moriori, the newcomers went on to kill 230 of the island's inhabitants and enslave the rest. Ngāti Mutunga and Ngāti Tama later returned to the mainland.

grandfather asserts that "I'm King Hunt, and when I say hang a man, hanged he is." He did not say that in my hearing, but was kindness itself, and indeed so were all the family to me.

My first acquaintance with Miss Hunt was rather startling. On landing I inquired about her father.

"Ah," she said, "Father's gone to Glory." And whilst I was considering whether to sympathize or congratulate, she further informed me he would return in the afternoon. Aeroplanes had not been invented at that time, so I could only express my astonishment.

Sure enough in the afternoon were to be seen − and heard − King Hunt and seven or eight of his great stalwart sons, coming down the hill from Glory Bay, on the opposite side of the island. Here a ship called *England's Glory*[58] had been wrecked sometime before. Hence the name Glory Bay. Thus was explained Miss Hunt's mysterious assertion. The men-folk seemed to be all talking at once, and were making a great noise, like children coming out of school. Children of the island they were, and children of nature, but true as gold.

We had for out entertainment in the evening the heartiest singing, which pretty well drowned the tones of the piano. This piano had been brought from New Zealand in the hold of a leaky old schooner some ten years previously. It had never been tuned, and for discord, I never heard its equal!

Next day, King Hunt came to me with a rusty old piano key and insisted that I should tune the instrument. It was no use my saying I could not and knew absolutely nothing about it, I was simply ordered to get to work, and either mend or break it. Accordingly, I set to work to take the thing to pieces, and by watching the effect of screwing up or slackening the wires I managed to get the worst

---

58   *Glory.*

of the notes much nearer harmony. My efforts were declared to be a great success, but some folk are easily pleased, and they are often the happiest.

Hair and fur seals frequent the adjoining islets, but we did not see any; there was also a large number of wild goats.

I had a rather startling adventure at Waitangi with a wild cow. I was walking along the path when the animal, which had been hidden by a bush, suddenly made a rush at me, and was within a couple of yards before I realized what was the matter. I was carrying over my arm a new pilot jacket with the inside lining out. This happened to be bright scarlet. I just stood still long enough to throw the jacket over the animal's head, which had the effect of bringing it to a sudden halt, and the jacket being entangled over its horns and eyes, was tossed viciously. I delayed no longer, made one jump and disappeared over the bank onto the beach below. I didn't think it was a laughing matter, but quite a number of the natives and others who witnessed the matadorian struggle thought so, and greeted me hilariously.

The Chathams were used as a penal settlement during the Māori war, and the Māori prisoners were employed making the roads. On one occasion they rose and overpowered the military guard and seized the two schooners in the Bay. They took possession of all the Government stores, but with their singular idea of "tiki-tiki" or righteousness[59], they did not harm the settlers in any way, though they were completely at their mercy. The mistress at the Accommodation House told me that she expected to be robbed at the least, and she put all her money and notes into a pot of boiling

---

59   Tiki-tiki: Corrupted version of Tika: Values that enhance and protect mauri
       (life-force) include, Tika: truth, correctness, directness, justice, fairness,
       righteousness. https://www.iponz.govt.nz/about-ip/maori-ip/concepts-to-
       understand/

broth to hide them. The prisoners all embarked on the three-masted schooner *Rifleman,* having tied up the captain and the charterer, and left them on the beach. They then disabled and ran the other schooner on the rocks so as to prevent the news of their escape being carried to the outside world.[60] Setting sail for New Zealand, with the chief officer as captain, for some time they had nothing but contrary winds and weather, and came to the conclusion that there might be a Jonah amongst them. Many were well acquainted with Bible stories, having been taught by the early missionaries, but like so many Christians of other lands, they often adopted private and peculiar interpretations of Bible passages. This is illustrated by the manufacture of ball cartridges from Bibles and hymn books, to shoot the Pākēha (white man) during the war. In this case they searched and found Jonah, a Māori who was said to have been a spy and an informant to the whites. He was at once condemned and made to run from stern to stern then to jump overboard.

Having thus satisfactorily drowned their Jonah, they had prosperous weather for the remainder of the voyage, until they arrived within "smell" of the land, there they took command from the mate, and knowing well the coast, sailed the vessel into a bay near Gisbourne(sic). Here they landed, with all the Government ammunition and stores, They handed the schooner over to the mate, with instructions to take her safely to her owners at Wellington, which he and the white crew did, glad to escape unhurt.

Taking their successful voyage as good omen and considering that they "stood in God's counsel," they and their friends then started on one of the most terrible and bloody slaughters, the Poverty Bay

---

60   Te Kooti Arikirangi Te Tūruki of Rongowhakaata (1832-1893) escaped with 300
      fellow prisoners from the Chathams, on the *Rifleman* in July 1868.

massacre, in which seventy white persons, men, women and children were killed in cold blood.[61] I visited the scene sometime after and saw the fireplaces and other ruins of the burnt homes. The leader of the expedition was Te Kooti, whose name will long be remembered in the history of New Zealand. He is said to have been originally a friendly native, but was unjustly seized as a substitute for someone else by the arbitrary authorities who considered "one n***er was as good as another." Smarting under the unjust transportation to the Chathams, he planned and executed the terrible revenge. Thus does injustice bring about its sorrowful consequences.

For the next few years Te Kooti with his braves proved a very tough antagonist, taking part in many fights, and never once being beaten or captured, although £1000 was offered for his capture, dead or alive. He was finally pardoned after the conclusion of the war, on his promising to live peaceably, which he honourably carried out.

On the return voyage to New Zealand the *Redcliff* started to leak furiously, which was surprising because till then she had been "as tight as a cup." On awakening one morning I was told that the men had been nearly the whole of their four hours watch at the pumps, and they were unable to reduce the depth of water in the well.

All hands immediately set to work to pump and bale, but we were only able to keep the water from rising higher, and the position looked very serious. We tried to discover where the leak was but could not find it. Then we shifted everything portable and as much of the cargo as possible, to one side of the ship, but still without success. Then we shifted everything to the other side, and listed the vessel considerably. Fortunately the weather fell quite calm, and

61   Thirty-three Europeans and thirty-seven friendly Māori were actually killed. https://nzetc.victoria.ac.nz/tm/scholarly/tei-Cow02NewZ-c27.html

we proceeded to bore holes in, and break out the inner lining where get-at-able, in the hope of finding and stopping the leak. The water in the meantime continued to rise and had quite covered the ballast, and there seemed to be no alternative but taking to the small boat and abandoning the old *Redcliff*.

It was then that I was surprised to hear a hymn being sung, and noticed that Holloway, one of the crew, had gone to the bow and was looking ahead, looking upwards, perhaps I should say, and was singing in clear though sometimes tremulous tones that beautiful hymn "Thy will be done." The effect on all of us was notable and seemed to bring calm and resignation to allay the excitement. Holloway to all appearance was as rough and careless as the rest of us, but he showed that a deeply religious spirit, and what is of more importance a will in harmony with the will of God, oft-times underlies a rugged exterior. I never hear that hymn sung but it recalls the scene, and I have since learned to know that to be able to say at all times truthfully, "Thy will be done," in the matter of one's thoughts and words and deeds, is to be a genuine New Testament Christian and genuine Old Testament Saint, whether with or without church membership.

For forms of faith let graceless zealots fight;
His can't be wrong whose life is in the right.

A somewhat similar case occurred at the wreck of the *Wairarapa* off the north coast of New Zealand when 135 lives were lost. Some of those who were saved were adrift for several days on a life-raft, and had almost given up hope, when a brave Salvation Army lass put new life and hope into the castaways, by singing that touching and beautiful anthem "Cast thy burden on the Lord."

At last we discovered the locality, above which the water was pouring in steadily. The inside lining boards were quickly cut away and the stream traced to its source. As the last board was cut out, a column and sheet of water about a yard high burst in, and a singular scene presented itself. On account, I suppose, of the sun shining brightly outside, and the dark interior of the vessel, the light was resolved into all its various colours in the column of water. This seemed like Newton's discovery of the solar spectrum by means of a prism and dark room, over again. We were all together, and what with the knowledge that we had found the leak and that it could be easily stopped, and aided no doubt by our intense fatigue, first one started a hysterical laugh and then another, till all hands were laughing heartily. Our mourning and all but despair was literally turned into laughter. Old Tim, the cook, remarked, "I've been goin' to sea for forty years, bedad, but I never seen a rainbow through a ship's bottom before."

With the aid of felt, tallow and strips of wood the worst of the leak was soon stopped. A heavy gale of contrary wind now set in, which lasted for ten days, during five of which we were "hove to." The seas ran literally mountains high, but ours was a splendid little sea boat, and when big ships would be burying themselves, and rails under, she would rise like a duck to a big sea with dry decks.

We sighted some ice just awash. At certain seasons of the year, ice drifts in from the Antarctic between the Chathams and New Zealand, and this, there is reason to believe, accounts for the loss of several of the "never-heard-of-more" wool carriers.

On account of the length of the voyage our fuel and all spare timber were completely used up, but we managed to harpoon a large porpoise, which we flenched, and made scrap of the blubber. This served for fuel for cooking purposes till arrival at port.

On the fourteenth day we arrived off the coast, and that night — a very dark night — we found ourselves surrounded by floating wreckage from the steamer *Ahuriri,* which had come to grief the day before. We managed to pick up some casks, cases and fittings. The skipper was in the bow, and let drive at something with the harpoon, but immediately came running aft, exclaiming, "It's a ma-an, it's a ma-an." One of the less alarmed of the crew hauled in on the line, and discovered to the relief of the captain, that we had salved a sack of flour. In the morning we arrived safely at Port Chalmers.

CHAPTER VIII

ACROSS NEW ZEALAND

At the time I made the journey overland from Christchurch on the east coast to Hokitika on the west, the only conveyance was Cobb's Coach, which in less than a day's run took us across the level Canterbury plains and left us at the hill-foots. The remainder of the journey was done on foot in five days.

The country at that time was little known; the Great Southern Alps had to be crossed, and there was no road. So the plan adopted was to follow the course of the Huranuie(sic)[62], which enters the sea on the east side, right up to its source among the hills; then to cross the saddle, and pick up the river Teremakaw(sic)[63] at its source, and follow it down to the sea on the west coast, and then to strike south along the ocean beach.

On arrival at the last sheep station on the Huranuie Valley we expected to be supplied with stores, but found there was absolutely nothing obtainable except mutton and potatoes. We were compelled

---

62   Hurunui
63   Teremakau

to carry a three day's supply, as there were no human habitations between the sheep station and the west side.

Fortunately we were able to add to our store by the capture on the journey of some Māori hens – Apteryx or Kiwi – distinctly New Zealand birds, without obvious wings. Their tameness and their intense curiosity made them an easy prey, by means of a running noose, on a piece of twine attached to a longish stick.

A great part of the journey lay through magnificent scenery, and between high hills. Consequently we had to cross and re-cross the Huranuie, perhaps fifty times, and wade in the bed of the river more or less for a good part of the way.

In crossing the Greenstone, the principal branch of the Teremakaw, for the last time on foot, the water was four feet deep, and running strong. A party of eight of us entered the river together, joining hands in case of accident. One man was washed off his feet, but we all managed to reach the opposite shore in safety. It was fortunate that we did go, as the river rose to a depth of ten feet in the night.

We reached the first store long after mid-day, and we heartily enjoyed hard biscuits, fat bacon and tea, realizing once more that hunger is the best sauce. One more crossing in a rough dugout canoe was made, and shortly afterwards we emerged out of the dark trackless bush on to the ocean beach, where walking was a pleasure, and the sight of the boundless sea most invigorating.

We passed through the Kanairies(sic),[64] where Dick Seddon was to be seen in his canvas hotel, dispensing liquors, and occasionally blow to obstreperous miners. He was so popular amongst them, that they made him Member of Parliament, from which position he rose to be Premier. He was an uncommonly shrewd, far-seeing

---

64   Kumara

and strong man, and earned the title of "King Dick, the uncrowned King of God's own country."

On account of the circuitous route followed the journey to Hokitika occupied five days. Hokitika stands at the mouth of the Hokitika river, on the ocean beach, and consisted at the time of one short street of canvas and wooden run-'em-ups, several stores, and grog shanties; it was a busy, bustling place, and rose rapidly to be a place of importance. Hokitika bar was the grave of many a coaster. I have seen six vessels on shore at one time; some were total wrecks. Yet those were golden times for coastal owners, and much money was made, freights being very high. I have known a small paddle steamer make £1,000 in one day, conveying passengers over the bar at one pound per head!

CHAPTER IX

THE *SEA SERPENT*

I LEFT Hokitika as passenger on the brigantine *Sea Serpent*. The night before sailing, the vessel had been allowed to settle down on top of her anchor, with the result that some of the bottom planking was started, and there was nearly five feet of water in the hold before anyone was aware. She was at once beached with a view to repairs. Next morning a favourable breeze for crossing the bar set in, and some six or seven other crafts that had been "bar-bound" for a long time passed us on the way out.

"Man the windlass," shouted the captain, unable to resist the opportunity of getting away. The anchor was weighed, all sail set, and we started, the captain remarking, "I've got brand new fly-wheel pumps and plenty of passengers to work them."

In crossing the bar the wind fell light, and the boat was sent ahead to tow. Suddenly she was caught and filled by a heavy breaker and thrown with great violence against the ship. Four of the five men were picked up, or scrambled on board, but the fifth, who had hold of a rope that was thrown him, had his feet entangled fast in the boat's gear, and he and the boat were towed astern through the broken water, his face being just under the water. He held on well, and was at last pulled to the surface and rescued, though much exhausted.

In the excitement the ship was left to take care of itself and drifted dangerously close to the shore. I ran and shifted the helm and she just managed to fetch off into the deep water. I received hearty thanks from the Captain, but it might have been better if I had let her go on shore, as on the voyage following to the Chatham Islands she disappeared with all hands, and in this was a strange coincidence. The brigantine *Cecelia* sailed by a Captain John Blair, brother of the Captain of the *Sea Serpent*, while on a voyage to the Chathams a short time previously, had also disappeared with all hands.

The powerful fly-wheel pumps were kept going about the half of each watch, till we arrived off Cape Farewell, where a smart jabble of a sea was running and here the leak almost ceased. It was supposed that the straining and working of the vessel had sprung the started plank back into its place again. In due course we arrived at Pelorus Sound, where the *Sea Serpent* loaded her last cargo of timber and then joined the numbers of "never-heard-of-more."

CHAPTER X

WHALE FISHING

Our two schooners, the topsail schooner *Bencleugh,* and the fore and aft schooner *Friendship,* were engaged in the coasting trade. The *Bencleugh* was a well-modelled craft and made smart passages, but the *Friendship* was an old fashioned bluff-bowed "serving mallet" and an excellent sea-boat; I used to love to make an occasional trip in either of them. We also held a small interest in the whaling barque *Othello,* and the barque *Splendid;* the latter was an interesting old craft, being a regular New Bedford (U.S.A) well-equipped whaler. Her six American-built whale boats were real beauties, the seeming embodiment of speed, efficiency and every sea-going quality, and yet apparently as light as a feather.

It was on board the *Splendid* that Frank Bullen gained much of his experience as narrated in the book "The Cruise of the Cachalot." I little thought then that he would in time become a famous writer, whose books are to be found all over the world.

Whaling ship *Splendid* at Port Chalmers between 1870 and 1890.
The whaling ship '*Splendid*' at Port Chalmers, photographed by
David Alexander De Maus between 1870 and 1890. Note on back of
file print reads "Whaler. F.T. Bullen sailed. The actual ship, given the
name of Cachalot in his book". Later note reads: "In fact Bullen stole
the logbook of the *Splendid* when it arrived at Port Chalmers! See
McKay Papers (Journal of voyages of Splendid) in ATL MSS section".
Signed Murray Bathgate,
Sept 1999.

Ref: 1/2-016340-G. Alexander Turnbull Library, Wellington, New
Zealand./records/22336328

Whaling in Small Boats.
(iStock)

I have found during my wanderings, many illustrations of the truth that rough exteriors are often no guide to the true character of the individual. Among sailors there are many men of uncommon perception and judgement, and literary ability is not so rare as some might suppose. The cook of the *Friendship* I one day discovered writing a bulky manuscript. He informed me it was a novel he intended to publish. On the door of a fish-curing establishment at Port Chalmers I saw a verse written in Greek by a very rusty-looking fisherman, and which was a skit on his employer. He had once been a college-bred student.

A chief officer once said to me regarding a young A.B, now Captain P—— , of a first-class steamer. "He is first class at everything, all kinds of sailor work, fighting, swearing, and now that he has gone on his holiness tack, he is damned good at that too, and lives up to it."

The voyages of the *Splendid* were, with one exception, never specially successful, partly owing to the difficulty in obtaining good, experienced officers. Several were imported from New Bedford, but the Colonial and Kanaka sailors did not take kindly to their severe discipline and "perswaders" (leaden-headed skull crackers) and misfortunes of various kinds repeatedly overtook both vessels.

The fishing-grounds were off the Solanders, Vau Vau, South Pacific and Australian Gulf. The cruise lasted from one to three years, unless the ship got full sooner.

I will endeavour to describe a day on board the *Splendid*.

The ship is dodging heavy canvas, a few of the crew are busy at various ship jobs, fitting and overhauling the gear, cleaning paint-work, sharpening harpoons and lances, serving rigging, coiling whale lines into the boat tubs, mending sails, etc., all in a slow and easy going manner. Suddenly from the crow's nest at the masthead is heard "A Blow-o-o-o!" Instantly the listlessness and apathy disappear, each man stops in his work, straightens himself up and looks around.

"Where away?" is answered from the deck.

"Four points on the weather bow!" is the reply.

Almost before the words are finished: "Stand by your lee braces" is bellowed out by the officer in charge. "Luff, Luff," to the man at the wheel, and then, "Steady, steady as you go, haul aft main sheet, fore sheets, jibs," etc, all which orders are smartly obeyed.

"Aloft there, what do you make of it."

"Looks like a small school of sperm, sir"

The ship is now "hove to."

"Man your boats, one, two and three," is the next order. "Lower away, shove off, pull three stern two, give way all." And they are off, each boat's crew vying with the others to be first in the water, and first to strike.

The chief officer, however, is generally first. The strictest discipline in the boats is maintained, and woe betide the man that makes a slip. When nearing the fish, there is absolute silence, the rollocks being muffled, and the boat carvel-built, that is, smooth-surfaced where waterborne, designed to make no noise as it glides over the water, propelled by five oars and a long, powerful steer oar. Grim determination and the lust of battle is expressed in the countenances of the harpooner and steersman, and earnest, if nervous, determination, to do or die, in those of the crew. From the stern to the tip of the steer oar one tension prevails. The boat and its occupants seem to be one live machine.

"Sparm whale, boys, sparm whale; lay me on to a twelve tonner," says the steersman in suppressed earnest tones, well spiced with the most emphatic expressions of various languages. Murder is plainly visible in his rolling black eyes. A "blow" is visible not far off, and the square head of the cachalot, like a huge black packing-case, appears, followed by the long smooth back and flukes of a sixty-foot whale. Then it slowly disappears head foremost.

The direction in which she is going has been noted, and the distance calculated where she will re-appear, and the boat is "layed" accordingly.

"Avast pulling," orders the mate. Presently the fish is observed in the clear water, rising to the surface just ahead of the boat. By a sudden powerful sweep of the steer oar, the boat is veered round, only just in time, for the head of the whale appears, followed by a cloud of vapour caused by the warm breath of the animal in the cold atmosphere. It is accompanied by a peculiar spermaceti smell. One has time to notice the small ears, the wonderful staring eye, and the barnacles attached here and there to the body.

The harpooner, having firmly settled himself, standing in the bow of the boat grasping the harpoon with both hands, leans well backwards, and then with one rapid thrust lets drive, aiming for the wake of the fin, in the region of the heart. The iron is well placed, penetrating the very thin skin, and about nine inches of creamy coloured blubber, thus being firmly embedded in the flesh. Instantly the whale "sounds"; round goes the bow of the boat, narrowly escaping the descending blow from the huge tail. Merrily the rope rattles out at great speed, soon sixty, eighty, one hundred fathoms[65] are run out, and the line is as tight as a bar; one hundred

---

65   Fittingly, "fathom" is derived from the Old English word "fæthm," meaning outstretched arms. The length of rope that reached across a sailor's extended arms was equal to one fathom. Sometime during the twelfth century, one fathom was officially defined as six feet. 1 Fathom also equals 1.82 metres.

and thirty fathoms and presently the line slackens, when all hands proceed to haul it in.

In time the boat nears the fish again, and when it rises to breathe, one or more lances, shaped liked African assegais[66], are driven into the carcass, whilst a second harpoon from another of the boats has also founds its billet, and again the whale flies from its pursuers. A careful turn or two is taken with the line round the bollard. The boat is towed by the alarmed and angry creature, and goes smash, smash, smash into every sea. To prevent the bow being towed under, the men, shift to the stern, all except the harpooner, who is ready, if necessary, to cut the lines with a hatchet.

Harpoons and lances are well placed, and the whale soon weakens, makes its final flurry, spouts blood, and magnificently dies. Where the irons are not placed in vital regions the play may last a whole day, and often the fish escapes, and the severe exertions of the crew are void. At other times it happens that the fish is difficult to approach; the toil is very great. A whole day may be spent in pursuit, and then not be successful. The weather may not be favourable and the boats may be drawn away out of sight of the ship. The dangers from a tangled line, a capsize, or an attack from a fighting whale, are always considerable, but the sport is the grandest in the world; the game is the most gigantic, and the value of the prize may be £800 or £1,000.

Guns and bombs are now commonly used in whale fishing, having the advantage of being able to be used at a much greater distance, and with less risk to the boats. They are much more effective and more merciful to the noble animal.

---

66   An assegai is a pole weapon used for throwing, usually a light spear or javelin made up of a wooden handle and an iron tip.

The ship *Splendid* holds the record for having caught the most extraordinary and valuable whale (Jonah's excepted) in the whole long history of whaling. This happens to be a really authentic story; one in which some respect may be said to cap all other known "fish stories."

In the year 1883 the *Splendid,* when cruising off the Solanders[67], captured an ambergris whale. Ambergris is a peculiar and very valuable commodity, found at rare intervals in the intestines of the balaena(sic) or "right" whale.[68] Some say that it is found in sick whales only, whether it is indigestion, toothache, or some form of influenza or appendicitis, the faculty have not yet diagnosed. At all events this animal was in very poor and sickly condition, with a very thin blanket of blubber, and no fight in him. He died easily, and was pronounced, on arrival alongside ship, to be an ambergris whale.

Except to chemists and scent manufacturers, ambergris is comparatively unknown, and many whalers who have spent their lives at the fishing have never seen it. Used chiefly for strengthening scents, and in the manufacture of Otto of Roses, and as a drug, it is more valuable than gold, being usually quoted in chemists' prices

---

67   The Solander Islands / Hautere are three uninhabited volcanic islets toward the western end of the Foveaux Strait, just beyond New Zealand›s South Island. The Māori name Hautere translates into English as «flying wind». https://en.wikipedia.org/wiki/Solander_Islands#:~:text=The%20Solander%20 Islands%20%2F%20Hautere%20are,English%20as%20%22flying%20wind%22.

68   Ambergris is a solid, waxy material produced in the sperm whale (Physeter macrocephalus) and also in the pygmy sperm whale (Kogia breviceps). (Not the Southern Right whale). It is however, only found in about 1-5% of these whales, so is not a common substance. Ambergris has been used for many years in the perfume and medical industries to fix the odours of scents. 'In the 20th century, synthetic chemicals replaced it [ambergris] so it no longer has much value.' (Rice in Perrin et. al 2002). But according to Clarke (2006) it is still valuable in perfumery as a fixative. https:// www.dcceew.gov.au /environment/marine/ marine-species/cetaceans/ambergris

current at £5 to £6 per ounce. It is generally found in small quantities of a few pounds weight, although the largest take on record at that time – some 200 years previous, off the coast of Peru – weighed nearly 1,000 pounds.

To the surprise and delight of all concerned, this catch of the *Splendid* amounted to 1,400 *pounds weight.* [69] At the modest calculation of £4 per ounce, here was a cargo worth £89,600! [70] Ye sportsmen of the rod, wouldn't you like to have a fish like that on your line to play with!

I was present at the opening of the huge barrel in which it was contained, on the arrival at Port Chalmers, and great was the excitement. In appearance it was something like farm-yard road scrapings, but darker in colour, with here and there cuttlefish beaks amongst it. The smell was far from aromatic, and not in the least like Otto of Roses.

The demand for ambergris in the capitals of the world was so small that when this huge haul became known the price fell to a very low figure, and it was several years before it reached the normal it is now again quoted at. Moreover, a large quantity of it turned out to be of inferior quality – was the "black" ambergris, and not the "grey," which is the best quality. The market being completely glutted, the

---

69   There are conflicting reports re the details of this ambergris find: "The bark(sic) "Splendid of Dunedin" found a piece of ambergris weighing 983 pounds and was estimated to be worth $25,000 which was located in New Zealand in 1883. "https://www.ambergris.fr/information.html

70   23rd December 1882: Otago Witness Issue 1622, p 15: In the report of the whaler Splendid's arrival at Lyttleton, it was mentioned that ambergris to the value of £3000 formed part of her take. We understand that one of the owners reports that the lucky find is far more valuable. There are several hundredweights of the precious material worth £5 10s per ounce and its value several tens of thousands of pounds. We hope the report will prove correct. Ambergris is used for making perfume.

imaginary fortune, like many another, was not realized, in spite of the ambergris having realized £4 4s, per ounce.

The cutting in and boiling down process during a whaling trip is a great job, and most fatiguing, being carried on night and day till completed. Grog and coffee is repeatedly served out to the men in most whalers. The whale is lashed alongside, the blubber is cut with spades in long strips, or blanket pieces, which are cut up, and put first through a chopping machine, and then into a boiler built in brickwork, with a furnace underneath. The boiling reduces it into oil in a short time, and the remaining "scrap" or waste is used to feed the furnace. The oil is then put into large iron coolers, and thence through a canvas hose is run into barrels in the hold. The skull or case is separated from the body and hoisted on board. It is often a great strain on the hull and rigging of the vessel, as the weight is very considerable.

The skull contains the spermaceti matter[71] which is carefully bucketed out into barrels. When the boiling down process is going on, the decks are full of blubber and oil, the scupper channels being plugged to prevent its escape. It is with difficulty that the men can keep their feet, and soon every stitch of clothing is soaked or perfumed with oil.

The whalebone from the roof of the mouth of a balaena or "right" whale often weighs five hundredweight and is worth £500 to £600.

---

71   Spermaceti, is a wax, liquid at body temperature, obtained from the head of a sperm whale or bottlenose whale. Spermaceti was used chiefly in ointments, cosmetic creams, fine wax candles, pomades, and textile finishing; later it was used for industrial lubricants. It is not used today.

CHAPTER XI

SYDNEY, RIO DE JANEIRO AND ACROSS THE PACIFIC

WHEN in Sydney in 1868, I was charmed with the famous "beautiful harbour" with its many pretty bays and beaches, with the picturesque city. We visited Botany Bay and the old convict settlement, where so much that is tragic occurred in the pioneer days. Many years later, I visited Rio de Janeiro in South America. Its harbour compares favourably with that of Sydney, and in some respects is grander. Our magnificent White Star steamer *Gothic* anchored near to one of the forts which had just been blown up with dynamite and lay in ruins. One of the periodical revolutions was then going on.

The "glory" of war, rightly interpreted, seems to spell ruin, desolation, legalised murder, and untold suffering and hate.

We then called at Las Palmas, and saw, amongst other interesting sights, the landing place where, in the fight, Lord Nelson lost his arm; and finally arrived in Old England after a passage of thirty-four-and-a-half days from New Zealand by way of Cape Horn.

When in Sydney I chartered the American barque *Ruby* to load timber at British Colombia for Port Chalmers. We left Newcastle,

N.S.W., deeply laden with coal, bound first for San Francisco. I was awoke the first night out by hearing the mate in a very exhausted and dolorous voice call the Captain, and inform him that his men had been at the pumps for nearly the whole of his watch, and there was no sign yet of the pumps "sucking." This was a nice awakening, to be sure. I got up and dressed, and I did not have my clothes off again for the four following nights.

All hands were at once put on to the pumps, and to reduce canvas, as a strong gale of wind had set in. The night was very dark; the sea had risen considerably, and the decks were continually flooded. The ship was on the last year of her class, far too deeply laden, and the top gallant forecastle and poop, in the language of one of the sailors, "worked like a blooming old hay cart."

Next morning the fly-wheels of the pumps were heavily frapped round with chains to give additional weight, impetus and ease in working. A deputation came aft from the crew, to request the captain to bear up to the nearest port. He at once assented, and an attempt was made to lay a course for Lord Howe Island. This necessitated laying the ship nearly broadside on to the sea and wind, and caused the decks to be constantly full of water, often to the tops of the bulwarks. It was then found impossible to stand at the pumps, so we were reluctantly compelled to square away for New Zealand and run before the gale and the sea.

For three days the weather continued without change, and the huge overfalling seas following threatened to poop the heavy labouring barque. It was found that only one man of the whole crew, an experienced old salt, and the chief officer, were capable of steering the ship with sufficient skill to prevent her broaching to, and being overwhelmed. So high were the following seas that the topsails were becalmed when in the hollow of the seas.

Meantime a life and death struggle was carried on at the pumps, the noise of whose clangour and gurgle and hiss remains in the memory of those who pass through such experiences. At every changing watch, both watches are tailed on to the ropes for a spell, and the wheels revolve like a steam engine; gradually the exhausted watch retire, and the speed slows down to a regular steady jog, interrupted now and again by a heavy sea tearing over the rails, sweeping and filling the decks level with the top-gallant rails, and compelling the men to jump and secure themselves on the fife rail, or in the main rigging, with a curse, a prayer, or a groan, as the case may be.

Scotch Alec, I noticed, always jumped for the main rigging exclaiming, "Oh, my wife an' weans." Tom Cass, a coal-black negro, was the least moved of all, and the only one who had any hope. He guessed he had "bin in as bad a fix befo'." Minutes seemed like ages before the buried burdened ship slowly rose to the surface, and the roll, clatter and hiss of the water, first to this side and then to that, seemed almost like a weary animated sigh of the sea, and return to life after a faint.

The main top-sail and staysail had been blow to tatters and about twenty feet of the bulwarks carried away, but no attempt was made to repair damages or touch a brace, or even latterly to sound the depth of water in the hold.

The Captain, who also worked at the pumps, had been hurt by being thrown against the revolving fly-wheel.

On the fifth day the weather moderated, an attempt was made to take a hatch off the fore-hold, with a view to jettisoning the cargo, but it was not found workable. It was discovered that the water was pouring in at the bows, some distance below the surface of the coals. The chief officer had himself lowered over the bow in a bowline to attempt to stop the leak, and was repeatedly plunged over the head in the sea, but could effect nothing. He had to be hauled on board again, when he remarked, "You *may* all go to hell together; I'm not going first."

"Man the pumps," immediately shouted the Captain and, all hands were at work again.

Next day, when nearing the New Zealand coast, where it was intended to run the ship ashore, it fell a dead calm, and after several failures to keep the hatchways open, we were at last able to start throwing the coals overboard, and succeeded in lightening the ship to the extent that the very leaky places in the bows, and in some other places, could be repaired. Being now above the sea-level the ship was free from water and did not have to be jogged out more than once or twice in a watch, except in bad weather.

> *We woggled on like a bundle of hay,*
> *And we set our teeth, and pumped with groans,*
> *And when we arrived at Boston Bay,*
> *Our arms were stretched to our ankle bones.*
> *Our hand were the size of Lincoln hams,*
> *Our eyes bulged out like the horns on rams,*
> *And we humped like monkeys bound for war,*
> *And every man had a raw red paw.* [72]

We were not quite so bad as that, but just felt that we wanted to sleep for a week or more, to recover from the exhaustion, and that

---

72   No attribution available.

we would not require any more calisthenic exercise for the term of our natural lives.

It was then determined that instead of "beaching the tub" we should proceed on our voyage to San Francisco.

CHAPTER X11

PITCAIRN ISLAND

Our next landfall, thirty days after, was Pitcairn Island, a beautifully hilly island and tropical garden. We intended landing to obtain much-needed fresh provisions and water, but a strong fair wind having set in, after very protracted calms and a long passage, it was decided to proceed on our voyage. In passing the island the scent of the flowers and fruits from the shore was quite tantalizing.

Pitcairn Island was first discovered and inhabited by the mutineers of the H.M.S *Bounty,* early in last century.[73] After the mutiny they

---

73   Upon arrival at Pitcairn Island in January 1790, the crew of *H.M.S. Bounty* discovered the island had previously been inhabited. Many relics of a Polynesian civilisation were found scattered around the island. The origin and subsequent destination of the Polynesian seafarers remains uncertain, although it is generally believed that they arrived from Mangareva, some 490 km away in French Polynesia...In 1767, Captain Philip Carteret's log, describe the first sighting and naming of Pitcairn (Ed, by Europeans). Due to 'the surf'...the Captain, of *H.M.S. Swallow*, was unable to land. Not having a chronometer aboard, Carteret miscalculated the island's position by 3° 24' and thus marked Pitcairn's Island 188.4 nautical miles west of its true location. http://www.immigration. gov.pn/history/index.html#:~:text=Upon%20arrival%20at%20Pitcairn%20 Island,island%20had%20previously%20been%20inhabited.

fetched Tahiti, and took native wives and then went on to Pitcairn. Three of the mutineers remained at Tahiti and were captured and hanged. The ship was run ashore in Bounty Bay and substantial houses, which are still in existence, were built from the woodwork.[74] The Captain and others were given the ship's boats and provisions and made a long and hazardous journey to Batavia and thence to Sydney. It was twenty years after the mutiny that the whereabouts of the mutineers were discovered; they had become quite a large colony, and were found to be a very religious and well-behaved community. Queen Victoria graciously pardoned the survivors, and permitted them to retain possession of the Island. They continue today a simple, natural and loyal people. Although there is little communication with the outside world, they are very pleased to receive visits from passing ships, and to exchange commodities.

Our passage across the Pacific was uneventful, except on one occasion, when we were overtaken when unprepared, by a cyclone. Nearly a complete suit of sails was blown clean out of the bolt ropes, and so great was the fury of the storm, that it was dangerous to stand on deck, and impossible to look windward and breathe. Wild, confused mountainous seas, whose white caps were fairly blown off from the top of the top of one to the top of the other, occasionally fell heavily on board. Two men were injured as a result and narrowly escaped being washed away.

The month of August in the South Pacific, and in the region of Cape Horn, is one much dreaded on account of the heavy winter

---

74   Fearing that if any European vessel sighted the ship, retribution would inevitably
      follow, the mutineers ran *H.M.S. Bounty* ashore and, on 23 January 1790, burned
      the ship. http://www.immigration.gov.pn/history/index.html#:~:text=Upon%20
      arrival%20at%20Pitcairn%20Island,island%20had%20previously%20been%20
      inhabited.

storms and we got our full share in making our Easting. For fourteen days we ran before a series of hurricanes, from S.W. to W.N.W mostly, which produced enormous following seas, old western sea-kings, whose grim resistless majesty and power threatened to scoop out our tiny vessel and crush her feeble framework into atoms. Captain Van Norden believed that the ship behaved better running than when hove to, and so she was kept before the wind and sea. She steered well in the hands of the well-experienced chief officer, Mr Rodgers, and Scotch Sandy, who alone among the crew had nerve enough, or capacity, during forty-eight hours of the worst of it to tackle the steering wheel.

The season was one of great magnetic storms and the Aurora Australis was repeatedly seen in great beauty. Words could not adequately describe the glory of one special display witnessed by us. The evening was almost calm, very clear and frosty, and the sea wonderfully smooth for those latitudes at that season of the year. The Aurora shone with most extraordinary brightness, so much that we could almost see to read by the light of it. The semi-circle in the Southern dome was at times absolutely perfect and every colour of the rainbow distinctly visible. Now and then the colours would twine and intermingle in glorious symphony. The immensity, the glorious galaxy of clearly-defined colours, the rapid kaleidoscopic movement and the silent grandeur of the whole scene arrested and concentrated the attention of everyone on board. An emotional wave seemed to pass through the ship's company, first surprise, then wonder, then awe, reverence and more or less fear. Then silence reigned, and except for the gentle swish of the sea, the rattle of ropes, the chafe and jerk of blocks and gear, not a sound was to be heard.

The Esquimaux call the Aurora Borealis, the "Merry Dancers," and say that it is the spirits of the dead at play. Certainly it is a most impressive sight, and when intelligently observed and considered in conjunction with the countless wonders of the deep, and the enchanting mysteries of the starry firmament, cannot but teach reverence (surely the foundation of any religion that is worth the name), and a respect for, and a desire for harmony with the will of Him who "humbles Himself to behold the things that are in heaven and also on earth."

> *Wonders in the heaven that's o'er us,*
> *Wonders in the earth beneath,*
> *Wonders in the sea before us,*
> *Wonders in the air we breathe.*[75]

The only other noteworthy event of the voyage was a fall of fine volcanic dust which came down on deck in a heavy tropical shower of rain, when at a distance of 188 miles from Manna Loa[76] in Honolulu, where there had been an eruption. I collected a quantity of it, and afterwards, at a meeting of the Geographical Society at Melbourne, compared it with similar volcanic dust from Krakatoa in the Straits of Sunda. They were remarkably alike.

The *Ruby* was a hard, hot ship for the sailors. The allowance of provisions "according to the Act" was carefully weighed out. The biscuit was more or less weevily(sic) and mouldy, the salt beef was very old and hard, like mahogany, and the substitute for sugar and butter was black molasses. The cook was quite incapable, and I

---

75   Unattributed
76   Mauna Loa on the island of Hawaii in the Hawaiian Island group is the largest active volcano in the world.

noticed the crew one day chasing him round the deck and throwing snowballs of badly cooked rice at him. It is a saying among seamen, that "God send food, but the Devil sends cooks." Several of the water butts had got stove in, and all were on short allowance of water. Fortunately we were rather better provisioned in the cabin. In a brawl between the Captain and the cook, the cook defended himself like Bailie Nicol Jarvie[77], with a hot poker, for which, and *pour encourager les autres*, he was triced(sic) by the thumbs to the roof of the storeroom.

A sailor's is a hard, rough life, and is often aggravated by tyrannical commanders. The wonder is that there are not more mutinies. A contemplated mutiny on the *Ruby* was fortunately vetoed at the last moment. Who it was who burgled the store-room we did not discover, but one is greatly tempted to excuse the culprits, seeing that they were suffering from sheer hunger.

On arrival at San Francisco, the crew were pinched and thin, and left the ship in a body, officers and men forfeiting every cent of their hard-earned wages.

---

77   The character in the novel, Rob Roy, by Sir Walter Scott.

CHAPTER XIII

SAN FRANCISCO

WE ARRIVED at the Golden Gate after a ninety-nine days passage, having come by a circuitous route, now never taken again. On entering the heads we were boarded by some five or six crimps[78] and their boatmen, who scrambled on board anyhow and immediately set to work to ply the sailors with drink and cigars, in order to get them to leave the ship, and to stay at their boarding houses. They were stuffed with lies about high wages and inducements of all sorts, and in the end there was not one man left on the ship, the crimps having cleared them all out, bag and baggage.

The audacity and daring of the San Francisco crimps at that period showed itself in the defiance of all law. One of the gang, well-dressed and with faultless linen, was hanging about the cabin-door. Captain Van Norden asked him what he wanted, and was informed with a guess and a drawl that he "wanted his sailors." "I don't keep

---

78   Crimp is an old slang term referring to a person who "persuades" (swindles) people into naval or military service. It can also be used as a verb meaning to do so.

my sailors in the cabin, go forward out of this," he was told to which he replied, "I take no orders from you." and putting his hand in his breast pocket, "An' I never draws but I fires." The Captain did not consider it prudent to continue the argument. These crimps had great control of the rates of seamen's wages, which are always very high out of Californian ports, and it was almost impossible to ship a crew without their consent. The sailors fresh from the sea, and eager for liberty and a good time on shore, were taken together with their dunnage[79] to boarding houses under the control of these sharks. They were well fed and kept supplied with drink and money. They were then often shipped away without their consent, for with the aid of drink, drugs and sandbags, the poor robbed, unfortunate victims were rendered drunk or unconscious, and woke up to find themselves at sea, with nothing but the clothes they stand in, the crimps having obtained their advance of two month's wages from the ship's agents.

I was most favourably impressed with the exhilarating and healthy climate of California, its magnificent products, the great extent of its trade and commerce, its wealth, and its enormous latent resources.

---

79 The belongings a person brings on board ship.

CHAPTER XIV

SOUTH SEA PIRATES, BLACK-BIRDING,
TAMATE THE MISSIONARY, BISHOP PATTESON

A FEW incidents from the lives of one or two of the most notorious of these South Sea pirates may prove interesting.

Bully Hayes, the South Pacific Pirate, as he was called, was a frequenter of San Francisco harbour. The following extracts of relating to him are from the "Life of Tamate," my cousin, the late James Chalmers, the New Guinea missionary.[80]

Bully Hayes became the most notorious character in the whole Pacific. Over six feet three inches in height, he was possessed of immense physical strength, and of this he was extremely proud. He was also a handsome man, with bright blue eyes, a strong nose, well-cut mouth, large moustache and long clustering hair. The most marked feature in his character was a temper, which, when roused, passed entirely out of his control. In these moments of ungovernable

---

80   James Chalmers (1841-1901) missionary, accomplished great work in Rarotonga
      and New Guinea, and was finally killed and eaten by the natives, at Risk Point on
      Goaribari Island, New Guinea.

rage, he became little short of a madman. His smiling face would assume the look of a demon; his eyes became almost black, and his face flushed into a deep purple. At such times he would do deeds of greatest cruelty, not scrupling to take the life of those who offended him. Possessed of considerable culture, speaking German, French, and Spanish fluently, his scandalous performances made him an outlaw in almost every civilized port. A sharp look-out was kept for him in Melbourne, in consequence of an unscrupulous fraud he played there on the occasion of his last visit. He had shipped 300 Chinamen at Hong Kong for Melbourne. At that time a poll tax of £10 each was paid by every Chinaman landing at the port. Before going on board the Chinamen had each paid Hayes their £10, as well as the charges for the voyage, but the knavish Captain had no thought or intention of paying over to the Australian Government the large amount he had received as the poll tax, amounting in all to something like £3,000.

When the port was within sight he contrived with the assistance of his carpenter, to almost scuttle the vessel, by making a large hole in its side. In an apparently water-logged and sinking condition, the vessel slowly entered the harbour. Hayes then had the flag of distress hoisted. Immediately the pilot and a number of tug boats put out to their assistance. When they came alongside, the Captain shouted, telling them of his sinking and hopeless condition. "For mercy's sake," said he, "don't stop to tow us to the shore, but save these hundreds of poor distracted creatures, by getting them to shore at once in your boats. I care nothing about my own life, if you will only save these poor fellows. Then, when they are on shore, come immediately for us. In the meantime we will work away at the pumps, and try to keep the ship afloat."

Accordingly the 300 Chinamen were transhipped into the tug boats and conveyed to the nearest landing place, which was several miles away. While this was being done, the hole in the side of the ship was closed, and all hands were put to work the pumps. Then, when the last lot of Chinamen had been taken off, the bow of the vessel was turned seawards, and away went the ship with Captain Hayes and his crew. He had managed to land 300 Chinamen, and yet keep the £3,000 poll tax for himself. It was a cruel business for the Pilot Company, who had to pay the poll tax themselves and were nearly ruined thereby.

On another occasion Hayes went to Auckland, New Zealand, and filled his vessel with a valuable cargo of cattle. He spoke of sailing on the following day, and promised that before doing so he would pay for the cargo. But long before morning dawned he lifted his anchor and slipped away.

At San Francisco a similar incident took place. In most parts of the China Seas, Hayes was not only in danger of imprisonment, but of death, as he had shed much blood in effecting his robberies. Prior to his last trip from China, he found out that his co-owner was wanted for barratry,[81] so he laid information with the American Consul, and had him arrested. Hayes then cleared away with the vessel as sole owner. When he found the doors of the world's large ports closed against him, he turned his attention to the South Sea Islands.

After the wreck of the *John Williams,* the missionaries, not knowing much of Hayes' history, chartered his vessel, the *Rona.* James Chalmers and his wife sailed with him 2,000 miles among

---

81   Fraud or gross negligence of a ship's master or crew at the expense of its owners or users.

the islands to Raratonga(sic)[82]. Hayes conduct till near the end of this long voyage of nearly seven weeks, was, largely through Chalmers' influence, everything that could be desired. Then in a fit of passionate madness he ran the vessel on a reef, fortunately without much injury, as she was floated off shortly afterwards. Hayes attempted to run down the missionary boat at Raratonga. They all had a very narrow escape with their lives.

Later on Hayes chartered another vessel, and went into the "black-birding", or kidnapping trade. When the natives came off their canoes he decoyed them on board, and induced them to go below and see the goods which were spread out to fascinate their eyes. He then had the hatches closed down and the canoes broken up. The kidnapped savages were carried to the Fiji plantations, or to any other place where he could get a price for them.

After a time British cruisers were put on the track of Hayes, but for a time he managed to evade capture.

The British Consul at Samoa was instructed to take him prisoner. Not knowing that he was in danger, Hayes sailed his vessel to Tutuila, an island of the Samoan group.[83] He went ashore in a canoe manned by natives, but before doing so, he thrust a couple of revolvers in his side pockets. The natives observed this, and when the canoe was half-way to shore, an unusual and unexpected event took place: the canoe was overturned and away went Bully Hayes beneath the blue waters.

The natives immediately swam around him, delivered him from the perilous water, righted the canoe and were profuse in their apologies for the accident.

---

82   Rarotonga
83   The largest island in American Samoa.

Directly Hayes stepped ashore, an effort was made to arrest him by Consul Williams. Hayes drew his two revolvers, and tried to fire them at the Consul but the powder was damp. The natives smiled and Hayes was easily made a prisoner. It was hoped that he might be kept till the arrival of an English man-o-war, but one night he managed to escape on board a vessel to some unknown port. Later on he was again traced. This time he was trading in a vessel he had obtained by fraud on the Torres Straits. Next we read again in the newspapers that the Mexican Government has placed the notorious Bully Hayes in gaol. Then we read that after leaving gaol, he was once more the captain of a vessel, but was murdered by his first mate, who attacked him with an iron belaying pin, when coming up the gangway ladder. Years afterwards he is reported as the Commander of a Japanese man-of-war *Haitchi Maru,* which during the war with Russia arrested one of the P.&O. Company's steamers in the Red Sea. So whether Hayes is alive or dead, no one exactly knows.

Another notorious character, who I knew well, confessed to me that he had spent a great part of his life buying old ships, insuring them above their value, and then wrecking them, with more or less loss of life. He had been repeatedly caught, and suffered long periods of imprisonment. The mania returned again and again, and even when he was an enfeebled, nerve-shaken old man, but he still retained the courage of a lion, and as little conscience.

Black-birding was largely carried on in the South Pacific, out of San Francisco and Australian ports, and was often conducted with great cruelty. Poor simple islanders were decoyed on board by all sorts of attractions and promises, as for instance hoop-iron, cotton handkerchiefs, beads, mirrors, knives, axes, calico, tobacco, and grog, and then carried off to work in the sugar-cane plantations of Queensland. Heart-broken by their treatment they died off like flies, and but few in those days ever returned to their island homes.

In later times, the Australian Government exercised strict supervision of the trading vessels, and obliged the plantation owners in Queensland to make humane provision for the islanders, and to return them to their homes at the end of their servitude. Each native is provided with a small metal disc, fastened around his neck, bearing a number corresponding to his name in a book kept for that purpose. These discs often get lost, or are exchanged, the natives forget the names, are landed at wrong places, and sometimes killed and eaten.

One of the worst cases known in this trade was that of a Melbourne-owned brig, the *Carl*. She had been cruising among the islands, and had secured seventy-eight natives. She was overtaken, after a long chase by Commodore Goodenough, in HMS *Rosario*. On being boarded there were no signs of the natives, although the hold was found newly white-washed with lime, and fitted out for the slave trade, with numerous ring bolts, leg irons, hand shackles, cooking pots, rice, etc. The brig was allowed to proceed. Shortly afterwards, she put into Auckland, New Zealand, short-handed, and reported that the chief officer, carpenter and boat's crew had capsized in the surf at Sunday Island, and all were supposed to be drowned. An enquiry was held at Auckland, but nothing could be proved, though the case was looked upon with great suspicion. Many years afterwards one of the crew of that brig, whose conscience would not let him rest, confessed what had actually taken place. It appears that when they found they could not escape capture, the chief officer and the carpenter of the slaver had shot every one of the natives, and the bodies were all thrown overboard.

The case of the *Princess* was another record of tragedy. When
at the Solomon Islands the natives seized the vessel, after killing
the captain and two of the crew. The mate and the carpenter took
to the fore-top with their Winchester rifles, shot and killed eleven
of the natives and wounded others. The rest sprang overboard and
swam ashore; two more were killed swimming. This was deemed
"unnecessary cruelty" by the captain of the British man-of-war,
who shortly after captured the *Princess* , and sent her to Fiji with
a prize crew.[84]

---

84   JIT glued clippings from newspapers into his personal copy of Voyages and
      Wanderings. This clipping from the the Otago Daily Times, 8th December 1928,
      is particularly moving and deserves inclusion. "BLACKBIRDING." SOME
      ADVENTUROUS YARNS. "Stories of the old time piracy and kidnapping of
      natives in the South Seas, to be sold into slavery, are amongst the adventurous
      yarns told by one of the former pirates himself, an Australian 79 years of age,
      who has just arrived here from a pleasure cruise in the West Indies (writes the
      New York correspondent of the London Daily Telegraph). His name is Archibald
      W. Watson, and he is a college professor now. He declares that in his youth he
      was a patriate, or "blackbirder." A price of £100 was at one time placed on his
      head, he states. After he went ashore, he studied medicine, and for 35 years he
      was Professor of Anatomy at Adelaide College, Australia. He says: I was born in
      Adelaide in 1849 and my life at sea began when I was seven. My parents wanted
      to make a child prodigy of me, but I did not like the idea, so I ran away. I was big
      for my age, so I did not have any trouble in shipping as an apprentice cook aboard
      the brig Carl which was then in Adelaide Harbour. I had no idea she was anything
      she should not be, but I soon found out. We set sail for the Solomon Islands, and
      the first thing I knew we were "blackbirding," or kidnaping unsuspecting natives,
      to sell into virtual slavery in Peru or the Guianas. They used to come aboard,
      when we dropped anchor, thinking they could sell us fruit and vegetables. They
      seemed so happy, but before they knew what it was all about, they were down
      the hold in irons. It was terrible. The poor fellows died like flies. Once we were
      away from civilisation so long that the war started, and we never heard of it. That
      was the Franco-Prussian war, and it was nearly over before we even learned it
      had begun. Another time one of the crew was sentenced to be hanged. His name
      was Frederick Frank, and he had killed the mate in a fit of temper. It was decided
      to swing the fellow, and a rope was run over the yardarm. Just as the hanging
      started, it began to rain, and the rope stretched so that his feet touched the deck.
      One of his friends cut him down, and he was smuggled ashore in a bag. I was

It was in the sixties that Bishop Patteson of Melanesia, with Bishop Selwyn of New Zealand, established a mission station at Santa Cruz.[85] On one occasion whilst Patteson was away on one of his cruises, a labour vessel anchored off the coast, and a message was sent on shore that the Bishop was on board. Seeing the Bishop was expected back by the natives, this caused no surprise, especially as a figure was to be seen on deck in a white cotton covering, which was a fraudulent imitation of the Bishop's vestments. Soon therefore, the canoes were racing to the vessel, full of light-hearted, happy natives, with a noisy, hearty welcome ready for their Bishop. No sooner had a sufficient number climbed on board than they were driven below and made prisoners, the anchor was weighed, the sails set, and the

---

cook on the vessel until I was 16, and then I managed to jump ship at Tahiti. By that time, I had seen enough of the sea, and so I got aboard another brig which took me to Melbourne. I then decided to begin my education, and went to Bonn, because I wanted to study in Germany, and it was the only name I could spell. There I met Joseph W. Warren of Springfield, Massachusetts. He saved me from committing suicide one day when I was feeling despondent." (Continued) In a handwritten note stuck into his copy of Voyages, JIT records the following from the Otago Daily Times 6th July 1928. Dr James Phillip Murray—"the man with the white skin and the black heart" was part owner of the brig Carl and chief in command of the blackbirding expeditions. For about three years he was 'resident surgeon' of the Invercargill Hospital in the early sixties. The Sydney Morning Herald 21st November 1872 tells of the trial in Sydney for the murder of between 70 & 80 islanders when the Captain and the carpenter were condemned to be hanged but Murray, " the most atrocious criminal of them all" having turned Queen's evidence was allowed to escape free though one of the witnesses stated that Murray stood at the hatchway firing at the natives with his rifle and singing at the same time "Marching to Georgia." In 1928 a "College Professor" arrived in New York from the West Indies who confessed to have been one of the crew of the Carl who was suspected to be the identical Dr Jas. Murray under the name of Arch. W. Watson and said he was for 35 years Professor of Anatomy at Adelaide College: Mr Mount, the "Bishop" passenger. New York Correspondent at Daily Telegraph 1928.

85   The Santa Cruz Islands are a group of islands in the Pacific Ocean, part of Temotu Province of the nation of Solomon Islands.

vessel cleared out for sea with her unholy gains.

Now for the sequel to this narrative. The real Bishop Patteson arrived not long afterwards, and the natives, smarting under the fraud that been played on them, and suspecting another trick of the same kind, instantly massacred the all unsuspecting and good Bishop. This happened at Nukapu in 1871. Later still Commodore Goodenough was also massacred by these same natives. His last words to his boat's-crew after he had received his fatal wound by a poisoned arrow, were "Don't fire." He died nobly, giving exceptional expression to the precept of the Master whom he followed, 'Love your enemies."

No doubt many a sad tragedy has been enacted among the South Pacific islands in connection with trading vessels, and whole ship's companies have been massacred. But the natives are not altogether to blame. They have often been greatly taken advantage of and deceived. Intoxicants and diseases, introduced by white men, have slain multitudes.

In some regions cannibalism and skull hunting still prevail, but in most of the islands the natives are not without noble qualities, of which unselfishness and life-long devoted friendship are not the least. An inability to appreciate the value of money used to be a distinguishing characteristic but this innocence is rapidly passing away.

CHAPTER XV

VANCOUVER ISLAND AND BRITISH COLUMBIA

We left San Francisco in ballast, with a crew of runners, that is, men employed merely for the run, and arrived at Esquimalt, the port of Victoria, the chief town of Vancouver Island, and thence sailed to Burrard's Inlet. The runners were a rough, unruly set, who insisted on "full and plenty" in the matter of provisions, and all their rights, and got them too, in spite of skipper and officers.

Our chief officer was an interesting person, having been a fighting man in his day. He was provided with a "persuader" and "knuckle-dusters "to keep the boys in order," and had had a strange adventurous life in many parts of the world. He had been through all the American War and was signalman on board the *Monitor* in the memorable fight with the *Merimac*. His description of the battle was most realistic. To listen to his yarns was great entertainment. The *Ruby,* however, had not sufficient attraction for him. He took an early opportunity to make himself scarce without leave, and in debt to captain and owners.

After purchasing my cargo of timber I had some £200 left on hand,

and was pressed to invest in land in the immediate neighbourhood of
the saw-mills. The Canadian Pacific Railway was only being talked
about at that time, and if I had taken Moody and Co.'s advice and
that of Mr Nelson, now Lieutenant-Governor, I might have purchased
the city of Vancouver, which at that time was bush land and swamp,
for a dollar or two per acre. It is now the terminus of the Canadian
Pacific Railway and a city of 100,000 inhabitants. But the golden
opportunity was let slip, and I was saved from what Mr. Carnegie
would call "the disgrace of dying rich."

I left the *Ruby* ready for sea, and proceeded on my way to Scotland.
Shortly afterwards she drove ashore in a heavy gale near Esquimalt,
but with assistance from two British warships, which happened to be
in the neighbourhood, her deck cargo was tossed overboard, anchors
were carried out and she was dragged off the beach. She finally
reached New Zealand in safety, but minus her deck cargo.

On leaving the straits of San Juan de Fuga, bound for San
Francisco, a heavy contrary gale was encountered, and the *Gussie
Telfer,* on which I had booked, was obliged to put back, taking shelter
in Near Bay, close to Cape Flattery, where we remained for four days,
till the weather moderated. Here we made the acquaintance of the
Indians, who came off in their canoes. They were just about naked
in spite of the wild weather. The skill and daring displayed in the
management of their canoes excited the wonder and admiration of
everyone. Only long experience could have made them the perfect
adepts that they were in negotiating the thundering surf breaking
on the beach. They showed consummate judgement as to when to
approach or recede from the towering, overfalling seas, and when
to sheer in alongside, one moment being level with the ship's rail,
and the next down at her bilges, for it was quite impossible to lie

alongside in their tiny canoes, or, indeed, in any other kind of craft.

Our first port of call was Portland on the Columbia River. The bar here in bad weather is often very dangerous, as the seas sometimes break twenty-five miles distant from the entrance. We were about to attempt to cross the bar, and were within a cable's length of the breakers, which after four days' westerly gale were running mountains high, when suddenly the machinery broke down. Sails were hoisted, but there was no wind; the anchor was let go, the stars and stripes were hoisted, half-mast high, cannon fired every minute, the life-boats lowered and an approach to a panic ensued. A large steamer, the *Ajax*, attempted three times to come out to our assistance but each time was obliged to put back. We lay in that perilous position from nine in the morning till four o'clock in the afternoon, whilst our very skilful "Geordie" engineer and staff effected temporary repairs. Proud and happy were all hands when we were able slowly to steam away out to sea for the night, and next morning the crazy old *Gussie* succeeded in crossing safely the most dangerous bar harbour of Western America.

The Columbia is a most majestic river, navigable for over 200 miles, with magnificent scenery along its shores. The quantity of salmon that season, both in the Frazer and Columbia, was almost incredible. Paddle steamers entering a shoal of them were known to leave a wake behind thick with dead fish, killed by the paddle wheels. On the way up the river we passed a large ship, the *Caller Ou*, bound for Liverpool with a full cargo of canned fish.

We left Portland per the *Moses Taylor*, commonly called the "Rolling Moses," and, the weather being fine, were able to sail close to the coast all the way to San Francisco, and to obtain fine views of the scenery.

Some of the hotels in San Francisco were remarkably good, notably the Lick House, and the Russ House (the Grand Palace Hotel was then being built), and the Occidental where I stayed, and where I saw Secretary Seward[86] and Admiral Faragut.[87] Faragut struck me as being a jolly, happy-go-lucky, dare devil, and as rather shabbily dressed. I visited the Chinese quarter, which is a world in itself, extremely interesting, but not a particularly pleasant or healthy locality.

---

86   William Henry Seward (1801-1872), an American politician who served
      as United States Secretary of State from 1861 to 1869, and earlier served
      as governor of New York and as a US Senator. A determined opponent of the
      spread of slavery in the years leading up to the American Civil War, he was
      praised for his work on behalf of the Union as Secretary of State during the Civil
      War. He also negotiated the treaty for the United States to purchase the Alaskan
      Territory. https://en.wikipedia.org/wiki/William_H._Seward
87   David Glasgow Farragut (1801–1870), a flag-officer of the United States Navy
      during the American Civil War. He was the first rear admiral, vice admiral, and
      admiral in the United States Navy. He is remembered for his order at the Battle of
      Mobile Bay usually paraphrased as, "Damn the torpedoes, full speed ahead", in
      U.S. Navy tradition. https://en.wikipedia.org/wiki/David_Farragut

CHAPTER XVI

OVERLAND TO NEW YORK

THE journey overland to New York by rail needs but little comment, seeing that now it is so well known. I have reason to think that I was the first passenger from Australasia to make the journey[88]. Through trains had just commenced running. Many of the railway arrangements were rough and uncomfortable, and several of the bridges were not built.

At Ogden in Utah Territory, from what little I saw of the Mormons, it seemed to me that they were a much superior type to the 'Friscans, but I did not feel tempted to remain among them. When crossing the Prairies we saw several droves of wild buffaloes, now almost extinct. In those days they were shot down in great numbers merely for the sake of the hides.

A luggage car caught fire in crossing the continent, and the whole broadside and much of the contents were burnt up in an incredibly short time. The passengers were greatly alarmed till the train was stopped. An axle of another of the cars broke, but no serious damage

---

88   1869.

resulted. We had great difficulty in crossing the Missouri at Council Bluffs. The passengers had all to be ferried across at dusk, with a gale of wind blowing and the rain falling in torrents.

I was much impressed with the greatness and importance of Chicago. When my mother was there in 1837 it was a mere village of 2,000 inhabitants; now it is a city of over two millions.

The Falls of Niagara impressed me still more; their awful grandeur, magnificence and power making the works of man sink into utter insignificance.

A fellow-traveller in the cars for several days was Mr. John E Vassar.[89] He had been through all the American War (1861-1865), chiefly with the Ambulance. His description of the battles he had seen, and the terrible anguish and sufferings of the wounded caused me to reflect on the utter foolishness, unreasonableness and wickedness of war. In this case it was a fratricidal war, though in a sense all wars are fratricidal, for surely a geographical line or a streak of water should make no difference to our following the commands of the Master. Did he not teach that all nations are God's children alike?

Help, help, help! Oh, God of battles, hear!
For the brave and the noble perish,
And our hearts are torn with grief and fear.
Help, help, help! sorrow, suffering, woe
Have overtaken us suddenly.
Wild war has come, with a crushing blow.

Help, help, help! strong men, torn limb from limb,

---

89   John Ellison Vassar (1813-1878). Missionary and evangelist.

With cursing, shrieking, madness, and pain,
Looting, and murder, and Death so grim.
Help, help, help! bloodshed, wreckage, and fire,
Hunger, thirst, cold, want, among millions;
Ruined homes, broken hearts, hellish ire.

Then thus I mused, God reigns through kindly laws,
Man must yield himself to harmony with those;
Discord and opposition to His cause
Rob him of his birthright joy, and cause his woes.
God rules through kindness, wisdom, justice, love;
Fools, when they govern, would abrogate His laws,

Set pride and greed and tyranny above
Right, thus awful war results, just from this cause!
What joy, content and ample wealth to all;
What rich and full development of being;
If War's vast misdirected power should fall;
And at the smile of Love and Peace be fleeing.

At New York, I handed over my luggage checks to the forwarding agents on the railway platform, and on arrival at the Metropolitan Hotel, in the Broadway, found my baggage there awaiting me, never having seen it, or had any trouble with is since leaving 'Frisco. Our British railway companies would surely do well to adopt the very convenient, safe and satisfactory method of the American companies.

I was much struck by the enormous traffic in the streets of New York, passenger and vehicular, and the tremendous bustle and hurry in which everyone seemed to be. On the top of a 'bus in Broadway one day, as far as one could see in all directions was a sea of vehicles completely blocked together. It was quite a long time before our 'bus-driver, by inches at a time, could force his way out. The progress was accompanied by chaffing, clashing, jarring, imploring, joking, yelling, and swearing in all languages.

It was at the time of the Fiske and Gould[90] railway and money panic, when fortunes were being made and lost in a day. I looked in at the exchange on Wall Street. To one quite unused to such sights and sounds, it seemed to be Bedlam, men being in the wildest state of excitement, yelling at the pitch of their voices, clutching at each other, many of them hatless, and in a state of *deshabille* with wild eyes and distraught faces. "Dollars, cents, green-backs, gold," could be constantly heard above the din, and that I suppose was what they were fighting for. The service of Mammon is to me like the armies and navies of the world, an illustration of misdirected energy.

---

90   Black Friday: Sept. 24, 1869, when plummeting gold prices precipitated a
      securities market panic. The crash was a consequence of an attempt by financier
      Jay Gould and railway magnate James Fisk to corner the gold market and drive
      up the price.

CHAPTER XVII

THE ATLANTIC AND RETURN TO NEW ZEALAND

I ENTERED America by the Golden Gate, and left it by Hell Gate, not having suffered the pains of Purgatory to any great extent, but having had on the whole a most enjoyable journey. Dynamite has been the chief force used to remove the dangers that attended the passage of Hell Gate in the days of old.

The passage across the Atlantic was singularly calm, and void of incident. A hooligan stowaway caused some amusement. He refused to work; said he never worked and never paid any passage money. Finally the hose was turned on him, but he only laughed at his tormentors. He was then shackled to a stanchion on the deck, and left till the morning, when he was found sitting with his hands free, having slipped his shackles. The only satisfaction that the chief officer, Mr Davis, had, was in giving him a good thrashing, and even after that he would do no work of any kind. Poor Davis, he had an adventurous life and a sad fate befell him at last.

He had been second officer on board the *Hibernia*,(1868) under Captain Munroe(sic). The *Hibernia's* propellor shaft had broken, an endeavour had been made to unship the propellor, but the broken shaft was withdrawn with it, and the water rushed in and filled the ship.[91] The *Hibernia's* boats were lowered and filled with passengers, and the captain's boat was picked up. Mr Davis in charge of his boat sailed over 200 miles to the north-west coast of Ireland, enduring terrible sufferings, which, most of the company failed to survive. When close to land his boat capsized and only he and four others were rescued. Some 300 lives were lost with the *Hibernia*.[92]

Davis afterward joined the *Europa,* and in the height of an Atlantic winter storm, he, together, with two other officers, was carried overboard with the bridge on which they were standing, and all three disappeared in Atlantic's insatiate grave.

On the morning of the last day of the year, peering through the mist, I could just make out the familiar Greenock Customs House. It reminded me of the two fishermen, who on another misty morning, thought they saw the same building, having spent the whole night rowing. They found out at last that they had forgotten to haul up the anchor, and that they were still in Glasgow. The authenticity of

---

91   JIT: A similar accident happened to the ss. *Harmony*, but bales of oakum were made to drift into the shaft tube by the resourcefulness of those in charge, the rush of water was stopped, and the ship saved.

92   28/11/1868. Accounts of events following the sinking of the Hibernia differ: The British ship Hibernia travelling from New York to Glasgow, with 60 crew and 82 passengers, sank West of Ireland in heavy weather after her propellor-shaft broke in the stern-tube causing a large ingress of water. All were initially saved (3 lifeboats and 2 cutters were launched), about 88 people went missing. One lifeboat with the Mate in command capsized. The lifeboat with Captain Monroe and another with the boatswain, 51 people in total were picked up by the sailing ship *Star of Hope*. The boat with the Third Mate in command was never seen again. One of the other boats, Second Officer Wm. Davies in command initially had 28 on board. Unfortunately it also capsized and by the time it was righted, only 3 had been able to hold onto it. They managed to reach Donegall after 12 days making the total of survivors 54. https://wrecksite.eu/wreck.aspx?146195

the story is doubtful, but the Scottish national beverage might be the explanation.

A very happy reunion with my friends in Greenock concluded the old year, and brought in the new, and once more I was home again in bonnie Scotland.

At the Glasgow Broomielaw, I found my old friend Captain Gamble, with his ship the *Dunfillan*. We had met several times before at ports in Australia and California. After renewed acquaintance with old friends and scenes of childhood's days, I sailed with him once more to New Zealand, and we had a very pleasant voyage together, with the exception previously mentioned, of the ship being on fire, and the panic that followed.

We passed close to Marion Island[93], and dangerously close to Kerguelen Land[94], the wind failing when near to the shore, but the current carried us safely clear. There were no signs of life on the islands at that time. Captain Gamble desired to make a particular examination of these little frequented islands.

---

93   Sub antarctic Island south of South Africa.
94   A group of islands in the Southern Indian Ocean.

Te Whiti-o-Rongomai. 'The Prophet of Parihaka'
– from a surreptitious shirtcuff sketch, 1880.

"Te Whiti and Tohu would not allow photographs to be taken or sketches made of
themselves...the best known likeness (JSIT used this in the first edition of Voyages)
of Te Whiti is that made by W.F. Gordon a Wanganui telegraph counter clerk, at
the meeting of January 17 1880. Gordon was refused permission to make drawings
and so 'jotted him down by stealth on my shirt cuff.' The picture was afterwards
photographed and many copies were sold. It was the first picture of Te Whiti and
showed to outsiders what he was like." (Page 207, Ask That Mountain: The Story of
Parihaka, Dick Scott. Penguin Group. 1975

CHAPTER XVIII

THE MĀORIS, TE WHITI THE PROPHET

HUNDREDS of books, from the time of Charles Darwin to William Pember Reeves, have been written about New Zealand, the gem of the South Seas, and of the riches and beauties of its 'Wonderland," so that I need only here remark that the climate is ideal, imparting health, strength, and elasticity to both body and mind. The scenery is magnificent. "Her mountains with their glaciers and canyons and cascades rival in grandeur the Alps of Switzerland. Norway has no finer fiords than the West Coast sounds; her geysers and volcanoes surpass the wonders of Iceland. Nature has lavished on the home of the New Zealanders all that goes to harden the thews(sic) and quicken the imagination of the race."

The famous Pink and White terraces of New Zealand were specially beautiful and unique. They were destroyed and completely buried beyond all hope of recovery in the great Rotorua[95] eruption.

---

95   Mt Tarawera erupted on 10th of June 1886. The eruption lasted six hours and caused massive destruction. It destroyed several villages, along with the famous silica hot springs known as the Pink and White Terraces. Approximately 120 people, nearly all Māori, died. https://nzhistory.govt.nz/eruption-of-mt-tarawera

Fortunately we have many beautiful photographs of them, taken by the Burton Bros.

I owned more than 400 acres of fine land in the neighbourhood of the Terraces which was buried under several feet of fine grey ashes. However, the grass grew quickly again over the debris.

The climate of New Zealand is superb and the death-rate the lowest in the world, ten per 1000.[96]

It is a sportsman's Paradise, game of all sorts and fish in a great variety being most abundant.

The principal occupations are farming, pastoral and dairying, but the manufacturing industries are now making rapid strides. New Zealand is rich also in coal, iron, and gold, £70,000,000 worth of gold having been exported since the opening up of the first goldfields by the white men.

The South Island of New Zealand contained at one time a large native population, but since the massacres of Bloody Ruaparaha(sic)[97] there now remain only a few scattered remnants of what at one time were important tribes.

The Māori population in the North Island is very much larger than that of the South Island, and on the whole is now slightly on the increase, especially in those kāiks, or native villages, where drink has been excluded. Drink and the European diseases have in many parts wrought great havoc amongst what is supposed to be the noblest of all the remaining uncivilised races of the globe. The Māoris have always been a most interesting race on account of their history, traditions, poetic imagination, skill and courage.

---

96   This refers to the European Death Rate as the Māori death rate was not assessed.
97   Te Rauparaha (1760s-1849): (Ngāti Toa, Ngāti Raukawa, Rangatira) prominent 19th century Māori warrior, leader and advocate for his people. https://www.ngatitoa.iwi.nz/te-rauparaha

In the course of my travels in the North Island, I visited the native village of Parihaka, near New Plymouth, where the prophet Te Whiti (sic),[98] famous through the length and breadth of the land, was wont to hold forth to his parishioners on his own appointed Sabbath days. He was supposed to be a religious Haw Haw fanatic, with a wonderful knowledge of the Bible, and an absurd misunderstanding of it. It was thought that he was stirring up another revolution against the white Government, but after events proved all this was a mistake. True, he ordered the roads that were being made by the military authorities through the native lands to be ploughed up, and the fences torn down, but his object was to keep his tribe as far away as possible from the deteriorating influence of the whites and also, if possible, to obtain the fulfilment of agreements made by the British, to supply schools and teachers to the natives.

Parihaka was a native village situated near the foot of Mount Egmont,[99] a beautiful conical-shaped mountain, 8,000 feet[100] high, the peak of which is generally covered in snow. A rough timber stockade surrounded the settlement, which consisted of about four hundred native huts, formed chiefly of raupo grass or flax, and containing a population of about sixteen or eighteen hundred.

---

98   Te Whiti-o-Rongomai was born at Ngāmotu, Taranaki, shortly after the second siege of Pukerangiora. He was the son of Tohukakahi, a minor chief of the Patukai hapu of the Ngati Tawhirikura branch, Te Ati Awa tribe, and of Rangiawau, daughter of Te Whetu. Through his father he was a second cousin of Honiana Te Puni and a nephew of Te Wharepouri. Te Whiti was educated at Reimenschneider's mission school at Warea, where he showed remarkable diligence in Bible studies. For a full and MORE accurate account of the life and mission of Te Whiti-o-Rongamai the reader is referred to "Ask that Mountain: The Story of Parihaka, by Dick Scott.

99   Taranaki Maunga, the original Māori name was reinstated for official use alongside Mt Egmont in 1986. Mt Taranaki has become widely adopted and Mt Egmont is rarely used.

100   8,261 feet or 2,518 metres.

Te Whiti's hut I found to be neat and clean inside, covered with nice mats, a small charcoal fire burning in the centre. In appearance the prophet is of medium height, well-built, with a well-shaped head, broad, but not particularly high forehead, and an intelligent face. The latter is kindness and good nature itself, especially when he smiles, though sometimes it is very serious and deeply thoughtful. I would suppose him to be a man of great courage and determination but without vindictiveness. During the war there was much fighting in his neighbourhood but Te Whiti would never take part in it and always protested against it, as being unwise, and contrary to God's laws. He distinguished himself by life-saving when the *Lord Worlsey* was wrecked near his settlement during the war, and prevented the massacre of passengers and crew. He led the latter into the British lines unharmed, together with some 20,000 ounces of gold recovered from the wreck.[101]

I was made welcome, and invited to squat on the mats. I asked him if he was Te Whiti, the Prophet, to which he replied through an interpreter named George Grey: "There are now no prophets. Now is the time of the blind, maimed and poor. I am the son of a man, no Catholic, no Wesleyan. I am only one; Adam was one; Noah was one; Moses was one."

"What about teaching of the Bible?"

"The Bible teaches family and tribal duty, and history."

"Do you believe all the Bible says?"

---

101   JIT: The Māoris have unusual ideas of honour or "tiki-tiki" (righteousness). Another similar instance may be mentioned. When the Māoris captured a bullock team loaded with stores and ammunition, as it was not considered fair fighting and "tiki-tiki," the teamsters and all their stores were sent on to the British camp untouched.

"Yes, except some parts which are of no consequence."

He then said that from the beginning there was good, and the opponents of good. There was on the one hand Adam, and on the other, the serpent; Abel and Cain; Noah and the tribes; Abraham and the tribes; Moses and the tribes; Joseph and the Pharaohs; the Prophets and the Israelites; Jesus Christ and the Jews; and now the Māoris and the Government. Jesus Christ from the beginning, and all along the ages, and Satan also from the beginning and all along.

He took a piece of charcoal from the fire, and drew a kind of genealogical tree on the clay floor, commencing with the three sons of Noah, Shem, Ham, and Japheth, and continuing till the present time. He then marked off the times of the Laws of Moses and the Prophets, David and Solomon, and of Jesus Christ, and showed how all through, there were opposing forces. I belonged to the house of Japheth, he to the house of Ham, but now was the time for all men to consent, and believe, and give all their mind to the house of Joseph, that is the House of God. God was his Father, he loved His will, and all might join the house of Joseph. Turning to the Epistle to the Hebrews in his well-thumbed Māori Bible, he read "his house are we if we hold fast our confidence to the end." Christ was the one and only door to the House now, and through all time past, we must be joined into His spirit. He himself was in the Holy Ghost all the time; he was the teacher, and he too was light, real light, and seemed to hint not only that he was one of the "Witnesses" of the book of Revelation who should be slain, but also that he was the Christ! He seemed to be very much at home in his interpretation of the book of Revelation, though it is quite beyond the comprehension of ordinary mortals.

I enquired of him, "What about the land over which the Government

and the Māoris are disputing?" After a pause he said: "The land
belongs to God, to neither the Pakeha (white man) nor to the Māoris.
You get an axe and stand with the House of Joseph." I understood him
to mean to take possession of, and clear unoccupied bush land. I was
struck with the similarity of his reply to Thomas Carlyle's solution
to the land question. "The land belongs to God and to the man who
tills it." Surely, surely there is more land in the world than enough
to provide luxuriously for all the wants of all its inhabitants, if only
men had the will, and enough wisdom, to remove the obstacles that
hinder the attainment of this most desirable state of affairs, which
would mean the abolition of poverty and want, much less crime, a
more honest, a nobler and a happier life.

Te Whiti further illustrated his historical remarks by the use
of a fern-leaf, its various branches being the various ramifications
of tribes or families, and also by describing on the floor a circle,
divided off clock-face fashion, into various stages, or cycles, and
ending up with wars, and the second coming of Christ, which he
seemed to expect very soon. I asked him if he would fight, but could
get no further answer from him than, "You will see, you will see."

At this time a company of soldiers under Major Tuke[102] were
camped within a mile of Parihaka and roads were being forcibly
made through lands acknowledged to belong to the Māoris. The
native village picturesquely situated under the shadow of the snow
covered Mt Egmont, surrounded by natural bush and a beautiful
river flowing by, was a most interesting sight. All of the old men
were tattoed, and some of them bore wounds and sword cuts,
mementoes of the late war. They were mostly clad in native flax or

---

102   Major Arthur Tuke (1831-1894) led the troops to arrest Te Whiti o Rongamai and
        Tohu Kākahi at Parihaka.

European blankets. They seemed light-hearted and happy creatures, but terribly tough customers in a fight, as indeed many of them had proved themselves to be.

As I left the chief's hospitable kāik, I could not help coming to the conclusion that Te Whiti was not the blood-thirsty rebel which the press and interested parties described him to be. I was convinced that he never intended to fight, and that by peaceable means only was he endeavouring to obtain justice and the real welfare of the Māori, and that he and his enigmatical sayings, his parables and allegories, which had so much alarmed the powers that be at Wellingon, were entirely misunderstood.

I observed too, a similarity in many respects in his teaching to that of Keshub Chunder Sen, the prophet of the Bramo Samaj, at Calcutta, who says 'be not Christians in the ordinary sense of that term; a mere imitation of Christ's virtue is not enough, advance to a higher ideal; *be Christs;* incorporate Him into your being, import Him bodily into your own consciousness, make Him your flesh and blood, assimilate his character, and let us all be so many Christs and let us all worship the Father."

He, on eclectic principles, sought to reconcile into one the diversities and contradictions of Hinduisim, Buddhism, Christianity, and Moslemism, holding fast to all that was good in each, but rejecting the objectionable evils belonging to each, as taught in the present day.

Shortly after this time, (1881) the volunteers from all parts of New Zealand were called out. There were 1,700 of them, together with the armed constabulary, and they were marched up to the Parihaka village, which they then surrounded. Instead of receiving them with weapons of war, Te Whiti sent out 200 of the children outside the stockade to perform a dance of welcome, killed quite a number of pigs, and prepared a feast for his enemies, of which, however, fearing poisoning, they were not allowed to eat, by their officers' orders. Te Whiti collected all his men in the open meeting-place or square, and gave them strict orders to sit perfectly still and quiet, and offer no resistance whatsoever.

The soldiers then marched with loaded guns. John Brice(sic)[103] represented the Government. Brice is the immortal hero of the now famous "seige of Parihaka." They had instructions to fire at once if resisted, but they were received with dignified silence, so great was the control that Te Whiti had over his men. The soldiers then proceeded to ransack the huts, to search for weapons and guns, all of which they took away, together with some Māori valuables, though this was contrary to orders. One hundred and eighty of the strongest and ablest were made prisoners, and deported to the prisons of the South island, where they were sentenced to eight years penal servitude.

Te Whiti himself was also taken prisoner, and, together with Tohu,[104] a Māori chief, was kept for one year.

The women and children and old men were thus left without their protectors, to subsist as best they could. The whole proceeding was outrageous and cruel.

The following is a verbatim report of one of the prophet's speeches. The Governor referred to was Sir Arthur Gordon, who in the matter of the "raid" was quite opposed to the New Zealand Government.

Te Whiti said: "In the olden times the line between evil and good

---

103   John Bryce (1834-1913).
104   Tohu Kākahi: Nō te iwi o Te Āti Awa o Taranaki a Tohu Kākahi (?-1907)

was clearly defined, but now it is obscured by artful reasonings, so that evil is made to appear good. This causes a great deal of trouble in the world, for although people try to do good they are often led away. To set things right they should listen to my words and try to do what I tell them, and they would not do amiss. God is not angry with the lowly-minded, but the proud man is an abomination to Him. Fighting is not the means God adopts to settle disputes. When the world was created there was no fighting. Love was the great source of peace. You should love one another and also the Pakehas (the white men). There are troubles at present for the Māoris but these will be settled by Him."

"We will not have War for a master – the loving heart must prevent that. Whoever differs from me is foolish. What I say may be all talk, but you are to pay attention to it. The troubles at the present time are like the confusion at the building of the Tower of Babel but that confusion will soon be settled, and the Governor of New Zealand is the man to settle it. Some people may sneer at what I say, but you are not to mind that. What I say is right, and will prevail. All people were created by God. I am engaged in teaching all, both wise and foolish, good and bad. If those in authority desire fighting the natives will laugh at it. Only God is good; although men profess to be good, they quarrel, and do evil works. We want neither fear nor fighting, to disturb us. All the trouble is nearly over. From the time of Babel, land has been taken by force, but love must now settle all disputes about land. Although we are few in number, yet we are great in land, and if we keep God's commandments, we shall take root and increase." Te Whiti concluded "All will be peace. There is trouble among us, but let us think all will come right. The chief of the world is the sword, but there is one sword greater than all – the

Governor. This is known by all. The Governor is the great man of the land. We do not seek to hide it. We are the most insignificant in the land; the Governor is the greatest in the land.

As illustrating the skill of the Māoris in the construction of *pās,* or native fortifications, the construction of the *Ōrākau Pā* may be instanced. Around this were dug rifle pits, in admirable positions, and masked with freshly cut ferns. As showing their invincible valour, a description of the attack by the British forces under General Cameron, and of the ultimate capture of the pā is appended.

With his soldiers, calvary and infantry, he surrounded the pā, which contained a native garrison of 300 men. Sapping[105] was resorted to as the method of capture. When after severe fighting, further resistance on the part of the Māoris seemed hopeless, the General called them to surrender. Rewi, their chief, hurled back his defiance in these memorable words, *"Ka whawhai tonu āke āke,"* "I will fight for ever and ever."[106] Hand grenades were thrown from the saps into the *pā,* and did terrible execution, yet the Māoris, with a reckless disregard of danger, stood up and fired right down into the saps. In broad daylight, chanting their appeal to God of battles, they marched out of the *pā,* as cool as if they were going to church, a solid column, the women, the children, and the great chiefs in the centre, having ceased firing, as the little ammunition they had left was reserved for defence in crossing the swamp beyond. They were pursued for a distance of six miles, and it is computed that 150 men were killed.

---

105   Tunnels or trenches.
106   Ka whawhai tonu mātou mō te āke, āke, āke! We will fight on, forever and ever and ever.

Referring to the defence of *Ōrākau,* General Cameron said: "It is impossible not to admire the heroic courage and devotion of the natives in defending themselves so long against overwhelming numbers. Surrounded closely on all sides, cut off from their supply of water, and deprived of all hope of succour, they resolutely held their ground, and did not abandon their position till the sap had reached the ditch of their last entrenchment."

CHAPTER XIX

VOYAGE FROM MELBOURNE

A storm-tossed ocean, what a spectacle it is! Born perhaps of a gentle zephyr from the cave of the winds in the South Atlantic, or from the calms of the Antarctic ice, the storm fiends grow in strength as they rush across the Indian Ocean, till at last they burst in a frenzy of tumult upon peaceful seas. They appear to be determined to crush utterly all that lies in their track; now like moving mountains, now like an undulating, rolling plain, they heave and wrestle as if in agony. Sometimes, too, they leap up as in joyous sport, only to fall back the next instant, hissing with a murderous anger.

It was upon such a scene as this, when on a voyage on the ill-fated *ss Otago*[107], bound from Melbourne to New Zealand, that I contemplated, standing in the lee doorway of the saloon house on deck, and wondering at the awful grandeur of the spectacle, and the fierce battle of the elements.

It was night, not a star being visible, and the sky seemed as black

---

107   The ss Otago was torpedoed and sunk in World War I. White Wings (Vol 1, p 155-156).

as soot, except for one singularly bright, almost fiery electrical cloud that floated nearly overhead. I had just come to the conclusion that the advancing sea on which I gazed was the mightiest I had ever seen. Like a living mountain precipice, it rushed on its prey, assuming an overhanging cresent form, into whose hollow we seemed drawn. Then instead of a crash and the fierce howling of the storm, there was complete silence, for I was buried, as it seemed, fathoms deep beneath the sea. I at once concluded that I was overboard, and as no boat could possibly have lived in that sea, that this was the end. I noticed that the temperature of the water was warm and pleasant, and that I had swallowed a quantity of hot, greasy or bilge water from some of the outlet pipes on the ship's side. It seemed as though my end had come, and many solemn thoughts floated through my mind in that brief moment of danger. When I regained full consciousness of my position, I found myself on top of the lee bulwarks, with one leg overboard, and entangled in the gangway davit gear. I scrambled on board, and up the sloping deck to the weather rail.[108]

The plunging and rolling of the ship had ceased, for we had been properly boarded by a very heavy sea, and having become part and parcel of the moving giant, were being carried along broadside, on the back of the huge carrier and so continued for what seemed quite a long time.

Away to windward like regiments of soldiers on a battlefield, or like a field of ripe corn in a gale, were ranges of crescent-shaped feather-capped, overfalling seas, the spume blowing from the one to the other, and cutting like a knife. Four boats had been smashed

---

108   JIT: Similar experiences of being washed overboard and then back again have
        often occurred, and are explained by the ship (being hove to at the time), drifting
        towards the man overboard, and, on the ebb of the sea, or the sea following,
        simply scooping the man inboard over the submerged rail.

by that one sea, one having been thrown across the decks into the other one opposite. Water tanks, hen coops, and every moveable thing had been washed overboard, the long skylight in the saloon completely smashed, and the house on the poop deck from which I had been so ignominiously ejected, as already mentioned, had gone overboard with all its contents. The wheel, and the man at the wheel aft, were completely buried under wreckage, and the wheel disabled. The iron bulwark rails were twisted and bent, the main stay carried away, and a new storm stay sail, bent for the first time, went away in ribands. A whole deck-load of horses, and all their fittings, went down at once, and the horses were bunched together in all sorts of attitudes, struggling and kicking in the front of the poop. The main decks were full of water to the tops of the rails and in the saloon the sea rolled over the sofas. It went down both funnels, flooding the stoke holes, while a great deal found its way into the holds, and on arrival at New Zealand many of the bags of sugar, of which the cargo largely consisted, were found empty, the sugar having been dissolved in the sea water. With spare sails and timber, the yawning companion way and skylights were battened over, but it was dangerous work. I still remember Captain Symonds calling to his crew on that occasion: "Work, men, work, and die like men, you can only die once."

Such was the power and the destruction wrought by a single sea. At such times, Jack swears by all that is holy that this is his last voyage, though he has to sweep a crossing on shore; but once in port he soon forgets it all, is the jolly sailor once more, and as soon as his pockets are empty he is found on board the first packet obtainable, and too often with a "Frisco outfit," consisting of a dungaree suit, two sticks of tobacco and three pipes.

A great deal is done now-a-days for Jack ashore, in the way of Sailors' Homes, Rests, Reading Rooms and Bethels[109], but much remains to be done, and many ports are entirely without such refuges. Some of his wealthy brothers on shore, over-laden with the good things in this life, might like Captain Cuttle, "take a note of it," and remember Jack at sea.

"Jack is a national asset of the first importance, being not only the carrier of all the necessaries of life for the British millions, but also, in the estimation of the patriot, essential for the welfare of the property at home." Non-patriots like Tolstoy and many others, hold that no streak of water or geographical line separates brothers, but that non-resistance, kindness, courtesy and love are the bounden duty of all classes and all nationalities alike, and that when such are practised, the Kingdom or reign of God is indeed within them, and His righteous laws are being obeyed. It may well be asked, why should His Kingship, His Kingdom, His laws and His spirit, be practically ignored and trampled on. Can His golden law, "Do unto others as ye would that they should do unto you" be improved on? Is not the law of the Lord perfect and all sufficient? Can it be doubted which will be the most powerful in bringing about the universal peace,

> *"When man to man the warld o'er,*
> *Shall brithers be and a' that,"*

Whether the Kingdom of God within, or Dreadnoughts[110] and

---

109   Bethel: a place of worship for seamen, usually non-denominational.
110   Dreadnought: a type of battleship introduced in the early 20th century, larger and faster than its predecessors and equipped entirely with large-calibre guns.

militarism, which is simply the training of men to kill each other? Did not Christ mean what He said, when He declared that we should "love our enemies," that we should "resist not"? Did He mean that we should hate, fight and kill our fellow-men? Yet this last which is War, the using of sailors and soldiers, whose quarrel it is not, to fight, and kill, and die, is justified by so-called Christian nations. Christian! After his name forsooth! Think of the appalling sufferings and cost of war, and magnitude of misdirected energy, which if industrially directed, would reduce the cost of living certainly seventy-five percent.

The total losses of France in killed, wounded and prisoners in the Franco-German war,[111] were 21,500 officers and 702,000 men. The cost of the war to France was £544,000,000. Germany's losses were 6,247 officers and 123,400 men; and her military expenses mounted to £77,500,000. The South African war lasted about thirty-one months. Our losses in killed and wounded amounted to approximately 44,700; and the direct cost of the war to the Imperial Exchequer was £211,000,000. The Boer losses were 4,000 fighting men. The Russo-Japanese war lasted for a year and half. The Japanese losses amounted to 135,000 men; and the direct cost of the war to the Japanese Government was £203,000,000. The Russian losses in killed, wounded and prisoners were approximately 350,000; and the direct cost to the Russian Government was about £300,000,000.

And as Andrew Carnegie says, "The immensity of the cost is as nothing compared with the immensity of the sin."

---

111   19 July 1870 - 28 January 1871

CHAPTER XX

VOYAGE TO THE AUCKLAND AND CAMPBELL ISLANDS

IN THOSE days of the "Early Settlers," sailing craft had been a very profitable investment on the New Zealand coast, but the introduction of quite a fleet of steamers, working for greatly reduced rates, rendered the working of sailing craft unprofitable and consequently new fields of employment had to be found for them. The *Bencleugh,* belonging to my brother Andrew and myself, was, therefore fitted up as a whaler and sealer, and I sailed with her for the Aucklands and Campbell Island. We got down the coast as far as the Nuggets, and the weather being contrary, anchored off Earlstoke, belonging to Mr. Wilson, and there enjoyed the hospitality of my old friend for two days. In beating down to the southward, the wind still being contrary, we very nearly lost the vessel. We had been standing on the inshore tack for over two hours, having previously been on the offshore tack for four hours, when I happened to notice in the darkness of the night a great bank of white breakers, and black, high cliffs that seemed almost overhead. I only said to Mr. Annesley, the chief officer, that it was time to go about, so that there should be no excitement, and possibly bungling, and then walked aft to see that the man at the wheel did not lose his head. Fortunately the ship came about like a top, clear of everything.

Whilst the rounding was going on, the cook, who a few weeks before, had been the sole survivor from the wreck of the *Wm. Ackers* at just about the same spot noticed the position and yelled out, "Good God, I'm about to be lost after all." Mr Annesley's remark to me immediately after was, 'Mr Thomson, the Lord has mercifully preserved us." It was within a mile or two of this point, that the steamer *Tararua* was lost with 130 lives, as mentioned in an earlier page.

A strong south-east current, and a heavy south-east sea often sets in at this point, and no doubt accounts for our experience in running our distance on the inshore tack so very rapidly, and also for the loss of so many ships on this dangerous part of the coast.

We sighted numerous whales in the neighbourhood of the Aucklands, but the weather was so stormy that the boats could not be lowered, and finding ourselves close to Campbell Island, we stood in and anchored in the well-sheltered Perseverance Harbour.

Campbell Island lies about 530 miles S.E. of New Zealand, and was discovered by Captain Hasselborough in the brig *Perseverance* in the year 1810. At that time there were no hair seals or sea-lions, but immense numbers of fur seals, and he secured 15,000 skins (see the MS. in the Sydney Record Office 1810). The fur seals are now quite scarce, and are supposed to have been driven off to surf-bound rocks and caves by the much more powerful and more numerous hair seals, who retain possession of all the good landings and sandy beaches. We erected try works, built a hut on shore, and explored the island; and when weather permitted, went boating along the coast in search of fur seals. The only inhabitants were half a dozen sheep, which had, we supposed, been left by the French man-o-war, *Vire,* which had visited the island four years previously in order to observe the transit of Venus.[112] I intended to have them shorn, as the four years' wool was about a foot long and a great burden to the poor animals, but soon afterwards we got caught in a gale which swept away all our boats and several spars, so that we were unable to land.

We found two lonely graves at different parts of the island, one of which was marked by a cross, made from a broken oar; the occupant of the other had been a member of the crew of the *Vire.*

We discovered two interesting caves. One was little wider than our whale-boat at the entrance, and left just enough room overhead for us to enter. Within we found a lofty dome and several beautiful shell and shingle beaches.

It was an extraordinary place; the peculiar light and colours, the clear still waters lapping gently on the beaches, and the silence, were all impressive and weird, and in strange contrast to the black cliffs and the noisy surf outside.

The other caves were a set of three, low-roofed, all communicating with one another. They were an accidental discovery. When cruising in the whale boat, a number of fur seals were observed on shore; we stood in so as to land if possible, but the seals, noticing us, made for the water, forming into a V-shaped column. I fired from the boat and killed the big bull leader, the ball penetrating the brain.

---

112   1874. The 1874 transit of Venus took place on 9 December 1874 (01:49 to 06:26 UTC). It was the first of the pair of the transits of Venus that took place in the 19th century, with the second transit occurring eight years later in 1882. As with previous transits, the 1874 transit would provide an opportunity for improved measurements and observations. There were six French expeditions including one to the Campbell Islands.

The other seals all retreated and disappeared in the caves. The only possible landing place was alongside a big sloping rock, on to which I jumped and promptly slipped into the deep water; but I managed, not withstanding, to reach the shore, with my gun.

Captain Moir and two of the hands having taken off their boots, and watched for a good chance, managed to land all right, with a second gun, and twenty-seven seals were quickly shot. It is usual to club fur seals, but we invariably shot them, one shot generally causing instantaneous death.

I had rather a fright on this occasion. I was on my knees near the head of the caves, in a narrow low passage, striking matches so as to see, for the caves were dark and full of gunpowder and smoke. I had passed an apparently dead seal, and was going for another just beyond me, when I heard a bark close behind. Turning quickly around, I found the passage blocked, and the daylight shut out by some moving body. I never doubted that I was being attacked by the seal I had passed, and whipped out my hunting knife at the double quick. Just then the match went out. I could make out a black head and sparkling eyes coming straight for me. "Kom outer dare," sounded huskily through the passage, and much to my relief I realized that Brown the second harpooner, a coal black negro, was talking to the seal behind me and dragging it out.

The seals were quickly hauled with lines through the surf to the whale boat, which narrowly escaped being dashed to pieces, having grounded on rocks in broken water. This was a good hour's work, as some of those skins were sold in London for over £5 each.

Ladies in their cosy seal-skin jackets seldom think of the perils endured in obtaining them. In some localities in the Auckland Islands, the sealers are lowered over cliffs hundreds of feet high, and then have to carry the skins on their backs for miles. It is seldom a season passes without loss of life.

We were soon alongside the schooner, which had been standing off and on in the charge of Chief Officer Captain Annesley, R.N. (who had accompanied us to the islands chiefly for the sake of the sport), and the boat was hoisted in.

The sea and the wind in the meantime had risen considerably and the seals threatened to take charge on deck, so they were made fast to ring bolts and stanchions. The very slippery and bloody decks were then sprinkled with ashes and coarse salt, to enable the men to keep their feet, and under small canvas we finally reached snug anchorage once more.

The appearance of the *Bencleugh's* decks on this occasion, with a slight stretch of the imagination, gave me an idea of the horrors of naval warfare, and vividly recalled to mind the slaughter at the battle of the *Chesapeake* and *Shannon*[113], as I had heard it described by old Jimmie Graham at Alloa. He and my father used to meet together to fight their battles and storms over again. Jimmie was a petty officer on the *Shannon*. He was afterwards captured and imprisoned in France, but, escaping to the coast, he crossed the Channel in a small open boat. My father would narrate how he had been chased up Leith Walk[114] by the King's ('God bless him') press gang, and how he managed to throw them off and escape, in the year of Waterloo, 1815.

---

113   USS Chesapeake versus HMS Shannon June 1st 1813 in Boston Harbour and is referred to as the Battle of Boston Harbour. Chesapeake sustained significant damage in the early exchange of gunfire, having her wheel and part of her rigging shot away and her Commander, Lawrence, was killed. The battle lasted ten to fifteen minutes, in which time 252 men were killed or wounded including the Shannon's captain who was seriously injured.

114   Edinburgh.

A tidal wave[115] overtook us whilst at Campbell Island, when all hands excepting myself, the cook, and the ship's boy, had gone overland to another part of the island. I had left the ship's side in the dinghy with the boy, and at once noticed that we were being carried up the harbour at a great speed. We were almost immediately at the landing, where the try works and the wooden hut for the shore-party were. We were then carried inland by the wave, which was eight feet in height above the high-water mark, for some distance, together with the oil and provision barrels and everything floatable. The big iron try-pot was floated out of its seat and capsized; while the men's hut looked as if it were attempting a somersault, the gable tumbling over on the brick chimney. As the wave receded, the house settled down again, but minus the two sides of the chimney. The boat was drawn back with the wave, grounded on the edge of the bank, and then it toppled into deep water and narrowly escaped being swamped. The bottom of the harbour was laid bare, and two longish, square logs were noticed there, the use or history of which I have often puzzled about since. For hours afterwards, the waves kept flowing and ebbing in an extraordinary manner, there being two distinct currents, one flowing up one side of the harbour and one down. This accounted for the extraordinary behaviour of the *Bencleugh.*

---

115   Most likely the tsunami JIT refers to was caused by an M 8.3 earthquake in northern Chile, and it first arrived on the main islands of New Zealand early on the morning of 11 May 1877. Reports of a "remarkable fluctuation of the tide" in Otago Harbour were noted in the Otago Daily Times, May 12th 1877. " The tide was observed to rapidly recede, and then as suddenly to flow several feet up the banks." "Through the telegraph, reports were also received from Napier (rise and fall of eight feet), Wellington (4 feet), Lyttleton (3 feet), also Waimakariri and Timaru, – Akaroa (8 feet), Kaitangata (4 feet), Tauranga (several feet all day) and Sydney (2 feet)."

She was darting about the harbour in every direction, twisting and jerking at her moorings in a most unnatural and alarming manner. The cook, the only man on board, who was an old experienced sailor, made sure that she was going on the rocks, and loosed her jib, cast off the wheel lashings and did all he could, but there was no wind and the steering was impossible. He finally came to the conclusion that he could do nothing, and that it was the hand of God, or the Devil, that possessed the vessel, the idea of a tidal wave not at first occurring to him. The two chain cables, and the two coir hawsers got so twisted and entangled that it took all hands next day, from eight in the morning till four in the afternoon, to clear them, and many of the links were worn quite bright by the unusual chafing and jerking they had received.

The weather being very calm, a most unusual thing in these "roaring latitudes" in the winter time, a singular echo was observed among the surrounding hills. The boy and I were occupied with the boat, salving the floating barrels and timber. One barrel containing biscuits was too heavy for us to lift on board, so I put my foot on the gunwale of the boat, and pressed it down under the barrel; then with a quick, strong pull together, we rolled it on board, at the same time as scooping up a few bucketful's of water. Thinking the boat capsizing, the boy made such a yell, that it echoed and re-echoed among the hills that surround the harbour.

The crew on returning from the other side of the island were much astonished to find that their whale-boat had been carried quite a distance inland, that the water in the harbour was like chocolate, and that there was a deposit on the pure white sandstone reef where they landed, of more than an inch of mud, caused, no doubt, by the action of the waves on the peaty loam of the sides of the harbour.

Many of the sea-lions have beautiful eyes, long whiskers and very pretty parti-coloured necks and chests and are magnificent, kingly animals, very different from the half-developed specimens to be seen in British aquariums. They are often to be met with on sandy beaches in groups of twenty to thirty. Sometimes they go inland for nearly a mile by paths worn in places to a depth of six feet by the traffic of generations. In walking in those ruts it was necessary to keep a bright look out, for one of our men got severely bitten by a wounded hair-seal – the first we killed. He was unable to climb out of the track of the seal, which he met travelling downhill at considerable speed.

Having cleared out the principal fur-seal rookeries we proceeded to cruise towards the Auckland Islands, and soon encountered a fierce gale. The decks were swept and two whale-boats and davits carried away, besides the fore top-mast, top-gallant mast, and jib-boom. It happened during the darkness of the night, and great difficulty and danger were experienced in cutting away the entangled wreckage which was dangling aloft and alow most alarmingly.

Dangerous overfalling seas caused largely by strong currents that prevail most irregularly in that region, kept tumbling on board. Two of the sailors were washed clean over the bowsprit, and narrowly escaped with their lives.

When the weather moderated, the main top-mast was sent down, and converted into a jib-boom, and thus jury-rigged and crippled we were obliged to bear up to Port Chalmers to refit.

CHAPTER XXI

WRECK OF THE *BENCLEUGH* ON MACQUARIE ISLAND

MACQUARIE Island lies about 500 miles S.W. of the south end of New Zealand. History records that in the year 1837, the Enderby exploring expedition was successful in obtaining a very large number of fur-seal skins here. The island has seldom been visited since. The position of Emerald Island is placed on the old charts as about two days sail further south. No one has ever landed on it, and it was supposed to be a rich fur fishery. It was, therefore, decided to send the *Bencleugh* to cruise in that region, and to land parties on one or both of these islands. Accordingly having refitted, we again started on the expedition.

Early in July, ten days after leaving New Zealand, we sighted Macquarie. A north-westerly gale prevented our securing suitable anchorage, and we got blown away to the south-east. In the ordinary course of things we should have passed near to Emerald Island, but this was not to be seen. It was a week before the wind changed or moderated. After having gone a long way south towards the ice, we sailed over the latitude and longitude of Emerald Island more than once, and at once concluded that it had either disappeared, or never existed.

Furious gales, with snow, hail and fogs, continued for three more weeks, during which we sighted Macquarie several times, but it was simply impossible to effect a landing. In one of the fiercest of these gales we had every stitch of canvas set carried away, while large portions of the bulwarks on both sides, the taffrail, stern bulwarks, and the wheel, were smashed to pieces. The steersman noticed the sea coming, and clasped his arms through the spokes of the wheel for safety; he was driven through the stern bulwarks and, but for the half of the wheel he clung having caught two of the stanchions, nothing could have saved him from being swept entirely overboard. So fierce was the storm that a single cloth of canvas in the main rigging served to keep the vessel hove to with head to wind.

A ludicrous incident occurred here. The broken pieces of the wheel were passed down into the cabin for repairs, it being quite impossible to work on deck. The staves of an American flour barrel were procured, the ship was ransacked for screw nails, contributions being taken from all kinds of fittings and furniture, and at last a really credible repair was effected. It was then attempted to pass the wheel on deck, but it was found too large to go up the companion way, so we were obliged to take it all to pieces again, and put it together on deck. We finally cast anchor on the lee side of Macquarie, after a weary month of almost continuous storms, with about half a dozen of the crew invalided by the hard work and the knocking about we had had.

We managed to find a passage for the whale-boat through the reefs and broken water, and landed one boat-load of sundries, including several bags of potatoes and some tools. We had just turned in for the night, when a furious squall commenced and our anchors began to drag. All hands quickly loosed the sails, and prepared to stand out to sea, but fortunately the anchors held. In the morning we found that we were only about a ship's length of an outlying islet, or huge rock, and had narrowly escaped shipwreck. It took the best part of next day to bring the ship up to her anchorage, and being Sunday no landing was attempted. A gale from the south-east then sprung up, and the sea rose rapidly. Heavy coir hawsers were attached to the cables, and led to the stern, and these acted as springs, relieving the strain on the chains.

At eight p.m., a whole gale was blowing, with fierce hail and snow squalls, but the schooner was riding to the decks splendidly, and taking very little water on deck. At ten p.m., wind and sea being worse, and occasionally heavy seas breaking on board, it was proposed to slip the cables and stand out to sea. On a consultation being held, however, and the opinion taken of the most experienced of the crew, it was decided to wait for a while in the hope of change, as the vessel was riding fairly well to the seas, and the anchors holding. At the same time the sails were loosed and stopped, and all made ready for hoisting. The straining and jerking on the chains became very severe, and it felt sometimes as if we were dragging, but owing to the pitch darkness of the night, the mountains being quite invisible, we could not tell for certain. At last a big king sea, heavier than the others, fell on board with tremendous concussion, and with the strain on the cables the ship shivered and shook throughout in a way to be remembered while out best bower cable parted. All hands were immediately on deck and the sails hoisted. I was standing at the foot of the foremast, and Henry Whalley close beside me working at the staysail sheet. The iron traveller which lies across the deck was one mass of bright sparks, caused by the chafing of the staysail clew, as, with hurricane violence, it tore along it, from side to side.

Suddenly there appeared over the bow a great white wall, which seemed to reach to the heavens – the ship was amongst the breakers. The second anchor had kept her head to the wind and sea, and prevented the staysail from being filled, and we were buried fathoms deep where perfect silence reigned, and the howling of the gale ceased for a time. Whalley was knocked down and his leg dislocated at the thigh, and one of the crew had his leg broken below his knee. Another had his ankle dislocated, and yet another was washed overboard, but entangled in the gear, managed to get on board again. I was lifted and dashed through the end of the cooking galley, and jammed amongst the utensils and broken planking. The whale-boat and davits were gone, and the second boat smashed; the decks had been swept of everything, and the hatches having worked loose, were stove in, and the ship filled with water.

All hands immediately took to the rigging, and very soon after the *Bencleugh* was writhing among the rocks, her last voyage concluded. Sea after sea lifted and jerked her about in all directions, the standing rigging began to give way, and the hull to go to pieces. Expecting to have to swim for it any moment, we threw off our coats and boots, and I was also hatless. The wind was bitterly cold, being from the south-east, and blowing clean off the Antarctic ice, so that the rigging was soon hanging with icicles. One of the men who had a longish beard had it frozen solid.

Meanwhile, the vessel had settled somewhat, the stern remaining firm, but the fore part lifting with every sea, as the hull was broken amidships. Presently a great mass of fiery white steam belched out of the companion way, much to our astonishment. Then the flying-jib was run up by hands invisible, and next followed the inner jib, both of which after a great clattering blew away in rags. Now came such a shower of hail, which seemed to be just great lumps of ice, that I and one or two others were driven to seek shelter below, and succeeded in reaching the cabin. The mystery of the cloud of steam was then explained; the water had risen in the cabin and extinguished the stove, which was red-hot at the time. As to the jibs, they had been forced out of their double lashings by the waves, and blown up the stays, where ice formed under the hanks, and made brackets, which prevented the sails running down again. What wonder if all became more or less scared and panic-stricken, for all the powers seemed to be against us! Besides nearly all were under the impression we had struck one of the islets off the coast, from which the shore could not be reached. I, however, had taken compass bearings of the headlands on both sides, and of the direction of that the wind was coming from, and noted that it had not changed its direction; so that I was certain that it was the mainland that we had struck.

Most of us went down into the cabin, and the remainder of the crew took to the cabin roof, covering themselves with several thicknesses of a spare sail.

The prospect in the cabin was unusual and rather dismal, the water being nearly up to the table top. Twelve men were standing on the seats, the man with the broken leg lay on the transom[116] with his face close to the roof, while my chest, which contained the ammunition and the only dry matches we had, was being washed about the cabin, together with a chest of tea and other sundries. The noise of the straining timbers, the continual boom of the oil barrels in the hold, which were all afloat, thundering against the bulkheads,

---

116   Transom: flat surface forming the stern of a boat.

the swish of the seas, as they ebbed and flowed in the cabin and sometimes rolling over the taffrail[117], and the howling and shrieking of the tempest, were all very alarming.

Little wonder that two of the crew proposed that we should pray to God, considering that vain was the help of man. This was accordingly done; very hearty were the amens; and the effect seemed to be to calm and cheer.

One would have thought that there was not much humour in the situation, but the various phases of human nature will out. The hatch of the lazarette[118] had floated off, and the steward, a stout little man, was crossing the cabin floor up to his waist in water, talking as usual, when he suddenly disappeared into the lazarette below, and presently bobbed up again, still talking away with his pipe in his mouth. This elicited the remark from one of the crew: "Lord! I thought the doctor was going up through the roof." Another of the crew kept on repeating at a very rapid rate the creed: " I believe in God the Father Almighty, maker of Heaven and earth," etc., evidently under the impression that a creed, a thing believed, could save, without the will and heart and mind being yielded up and made subject to the Kingdom and reign of God within. Similarly, many a disastrous shipwreck has resulted from the shipmaster *believing* that he was on a safe course, when an alerting movement of the helm (and nothing else) would have brought salvation. Belief is no saviour, but "'bout ship" (which is repentance), with the spirit of Christ the new Captain of Salvation admitted and in command, does bring salvation from all wrong thinking and wrong doing and dispels the fears of the battle of life, of death, and of hereafter.

---

117   Taffrail: the rail around a ship's stern.
118   Rear of the ship's hold.

At last the day broke, and with it came the comforting discovery that we had not struck the adjacent small islands, from where there would have been no escape, but a reef of rugged rocks, a considerable distance from the shore. Fortunately the vessel had been driven into a natural dock, or cleft in the reef, stern first, and lay head to sea, the latter rolling up the decks and over the taffrail. Had she struck a few yards on either side, she would have fallen broadside on and none probably would have been left to tell the tale.

From the tops of the mountains to the black rocks at the water's edge, fringed everywhere by the crashing breakers, was a thick coverage of snow. The beach was strewn with wreckage, the remains of two boats, oars, barrels, etc., and a long great fringe of seaweed, some of it fifty feet long, kept lashing the rocky shore.

Standing solitary in the great waste of stormy waters, this white smooth, mountainous island seemed to me like some monstrous animal couchant, and about to spring, in deadly combat with the fierce eternal elements, and all the wild forces of the universe.

How to reach the shore was the problem that now faced us. All our boats were gone, broken reefs of rock with deep water here and there, lay between us and the land with deep water here and there, lay between us and the land, breakers continued constantly, though the hull formed a kind of breakwater, and smoothed the seas to some extent. The long lengths of ever-restless seaweed seemed very dangerous entanglements. Captain Bezer called for volunteers to take a line to the shore, and two men at once responded. Delay was urged for various reasons, and finally the captain declared that he would go himself. The day was advancing and the days are very short at that time of year, being mid-winter, so, as there was no sign of an attempt being made, and feeling burdened with the responsibility of the position, I considered it my duty to make the attempt, which, after all, proved not so difficult as it seemed. I watched for some time for a "smooth" after three heavy seas, and then slid down a rope over the stern. My first attempt was a signal failure, as I let go too soon, expecting to be able to overcome the last of the ebb of the receding wave; and I was carried under the ship's counter, and then alongside to near the fore-rigging, but was hauled back on the incoming sea by the small line I had fastened under my arms to take on shore. I thus managed at last to get to the bowline again that hung from the stern.

I started again at the next chance, and helped by the hearty encouragements of my shipmates, and a life buoy which was thrown after me, I succeeded in reaching the shore without much swimming. My greatest difficulty was the long, snaky seaweed, which threatened both to over-power me, and to entangle the line. A thick rope was then made fast to the small line, hauled on shore and the end made fast to a rock. The rope was hove taut, and one of the sailors managed to come ashore by means of it. Finally on a bowline, as a substitute for a boatswain's chair, with blocks and running gear fitted up, by means of which the whole crew was safely landed. The captain said on landing, that, when slung in the bowline, with the seas hissing and thundering beneath him, he could not for a time understand where he was, or what was happening.

Shipwrecked, stranded on one of the most desolate islands in the world, close to the Antarctic, some of us without coats, hats and shoes, two men with broken legs, and several others injured, all of us wet, weary, sleepy and hungry, we formed a curious picture. The background consisted of pure white snowy hills, while in the foreground was the black, rocky, hissing beach, the breakers and all that remained of my favourite schooner.

Of the latter the usually trim masts and yards were all awry, clustered with icicles. These were not, as one would expect, all hanging perpendicularly, but many were standing out horizontally like pennants, so great had been the force of the wind, and the intensity of the frost. The tatters of the head sails were still cracking in the breeze, each hank supported by a bracket of ice. The bulwarks having gone, the decks were being swept by the seas. The rudder was gone and here and there in the planking were great holes, through which the waves ebbed and flowed. The whole ship was in constant movement, like the last dying agony of a living creature.

With considerable difficulty we struggled along the beach; I myself stumbled and fell repeatedly, and my wet clothes had become frozen hard. At last we reached the two old wooden huts which had been left very many years ago, by previous residents on the island. They were in a most dilapidated condition, but we were exceedingly glad to get into shelter and out of the cold wind, and we soon had a fire going, before which we became somewhat thawed, if not dried.

All that day we had nothing to eat, excepting a teacupful each of preserved soup, a few tins of which together with a tin of coffee, had been brought ashore from the ship. There being no water obtainable, snow was melted from the front of the hut, but the spray from the storm had been flying over the roof, and this made the snow, and consequently the coffee, quite salt. Still, it did not prevent us from drinking it, and it seemed it seemed to put new life into us. Two galvanised buckets in which we made the coffee, and which had been landed on the Saturday, together with several bags of potatoes, were found most useful. They were filled with potatoes and put on to boil, and we congratulated ourselves that we were going to have a good feed, and that we could not starve as long as they lasted. They were boiled for half an hour and did not soften, and then for another half an hour, with the same result; and then longer still. We blamed the bad fire, till at last it dawned on us that they were frosted and so they proved perfectly uneatable. Great then was our disappointment!

The hut of which Captain Bezer, the steward and I, had taken possession measured eight feet by ten feet, and contained two bunks. The captain and I got into one, but it was so narrow that we had to lie on our sides, and then couldn't move, but it helped together with the substantial personality of the captain to increase the warmth. Being utterly exhausted I slept and rested, in spite of the hard boards and the absence of both bedding and covering.

Next morning our great anxiety was to get something to eat, and some clothes. We started down the beach like the hungry wreckers that we were, to see what we could pick up. The only thing we found to eat that day was a half-sack of pearl barley, sodden with salt water but still quite good to eat. Bucketful after bucketful was boiled till late into the night, as there seemed to be no satisfying our hunger. We added to it a little ancient liquid sugar, which was found in a keg in one of the huts and it proved most palatable and strengthening. I have had great respect for barley ever since, for it really put new strength into all of us.

Henry Whalley[119], our chief harpooner, whose leg was broken

---

119   Henry was the son of Robert "Governor" Wallen, a pioneer of Kangaroo Island
       and one of his aboriginal (Palawa) "wives." Henry grew up on his family's farm
       at Three Wells River (now Cygnet River) Kangaroo Island, where his parents
       hunted animal skins. These they traded with passing ships, along with fresh
       produce from the farm. The business did well enough for his father to send
       Henry to Hobart Town to receive an education. Henry took the surname Whalley
       and joined whaling ships where he was known as Harry or Black Harry Whalley.

or dislocated close to the body, died the night after the wreck. Fortunately he suffered little, as he was quite benumbed and seemed to have lost feeling in his limbs. He had a drink of hot coffee and remarked, "That is good; now I will have a long sleep." Shortly after when his henchman, young George Baker, turned to see him, he found that he was indeed having his long sleep, and that life had departed.

Baker and Whalley were both from Tasmania, and were much attached to each other. It was those two who on a previous voyage had gone aloft in a heavy gale, on a very dark night, at the risk of their lives, to cut away the wreckage of the fore-topmast and all the yards and gear, which like a huge steel spider's web, were swinging in mid-air, smashing up and destroying everything. Whalley was a singular man; his father, he told me, was the captain of an American whaler, and his mother the very last of the Tasmanian natives, closely related to King Billy, the last of them all. He had seen a good deal of convict life, when Tasmania was a convict settlement, and had had strange experiences. Much of his chequered life was spent in whaling in the wild days, when drunken orgies and violence among the natives and the sailors were quite customary. He had a kindly and cheerful disposition, and was a great favourite with all on board, being possessed of great courage and self-reliance. He once said to me when I was admiring some specially natty sailor work which I found him doing, "Misi Thomson" (the natives could not pronounce

One of his shipmates on the Runnymede was William Lanne or Lanney (King Billy), who was the last full-blood male Tasmanian aboriginal (Palawa) and said to be a close relative of Henry's mother. In March 1869 Henry was a pall-bearer at Lanne's funeral. Henry died in August 1877 at age 58. https://www.wikitree.com/wiki/Wallen-427

the letter *r*) "a good man can do anything he makes his mind to do, no matter what." And the recollection of this has rallied me when in hard places more than once.

With some difficulty we managed to dig a grave about five feet deep, when to our surprise, we came on the ribs of a vessel, an unknown waif of the sea, which must have been buried up with shingle by the action of waves in ages past. Bearing a most placid smile, Whalley was gently laid in the old wreck, his shipmates standing by to take leave of him. One of the crew asked permission to repeat the Church of England burial service. This he did with much apparent reverence and feeling, and with faultless intonation. Several armfuls of then pure white snow served to cover him up, and then the grave was filled up with earth. A panel from the walls of *Bencleugh's* cabin, fitted to an iron standard, served as a headstone, and to this was attached the folding log-slate of the schooner, with an obituary notice deeply scratched into it.

> *There calmly let him sleep.*
> *Not all the winds that blow*
> *Can shake his bed, and he shall keep*
> *A quiet watch below.*

There grew on his grave one beautiful little blue flower, like a lobelia, the only flower which we observed on the desolate island.

The sailor who had repeated the burial service, practically as well as any man-ordained parson, was only known by the name of Cockney. I tried to find out something about him, but all that he would admit was that "Lunnon town" was too "hot" to hold him, and that he came to the Colonies for a change of air. Amongst the strange medley of characters in our crew, each with a history of his own, he was perhaps the most interesting. He and the mate were the only persons who recovered their kit bags containing their clothes. Cockney at once divided his amongst the most necessitous of the crew. The mate being that kind of a Scotsman who keeps the Sabbath and everything else besides, insisted on keeping his own, but finally had to yield to the barracking of the others, and divided his also.

Next day Baker and I managed to get on the wreck by means of the boatswain's chair, and our first search was for something to eat. A solitary biscuit, sodden with salt water, and the contents of a half-empty sugar basin was all that we found. We managed to break out half a box of tinned meat, some tins of coffee, and half a pack of split peas, all of which were received on shore with great delight. I also took one of my bedsheets, which was wanted for bandages, and the medicine chest, containing some cotton wool. Meantime the barrels which had been washed ashore were carefully overhauled, and flour and biscuits discovered amongst them. It was found that neither the Captain nor anyone else knew anything about setting broken legs, but the invalid and his chums had held a consultation and concluded that the leg should be " 'fished,' same's a broken spar, sir." Accordingly two rough splints were whittled out of the shape of the leg, and by squeezing and pulling about the broken limb, it was made to correspond in shape and appearance with the other one, the poor victim in the meantime suffering considerably from the rough, ignorant treatment. Cotton stuffing was laid under the splints, and then a taut servicing of bandage. The invalid was then informed that it would soon be stronger than the other one. The reason was as follows: " 'Cause why, you can fish a spar and make it stronger than it ever was, and why not a broken leg? Yuss I'll back Pentney against any of yees, in a race on the beach bye-and-bye." Fortunately Pentney was a strong healthy man, and the break was in a good place, and he made a rapid recovery, a peculiarity being that he slept tremendously, the men said twenty hours out of twenty-four regularly.

The next anxiety was to save as much as possible from the wreck, before anything more got washed out to sea. Accordingly all the remaining sails were unbent, and cut up for blankets, and for covering the huts, which at one time had been covered with sea-elephant skins, which were now completely decayed. Some of the blankets from the cabin were recovered, and distributed as far as they would go, and all the oil and other casks that could be reached were hauled on shore. A number of them were found to contain biscuits, flour, and oatmeal, in good condition; others were stove in, and immediately the contents went mouldy and a good many went out to sea.

Some sugar, a chest of tea, the greater part of which would soon become mouldy, a whole box of tobacco, which caused much rejoicing, a rifle, two double-barrelled fowling-pieces, and some ammunition, were also salved and stored in the Captain's hut, and to the honour of all concerned, though the temptation was great, there was little pilfering.

THE HUTS, MACQUARIE ISLAND.

The Huts on Macquarie Island
(Drawing by J. Inches Thomson)

139

CHAPTER XXII

LIFE ON THE DESERT ISLAND

Having taken note of our provisions and housed them as well as circumstances would permit, we proceeded to make the huts as comfortable as possible. As soon as the frost would allow, trenches were cut for drainage, and a floor laid down, which consisted of the hatches of the *Bencleugh*. Our shack was dignified by the name of the cabin and was occupied by Captain Bezer, myself and the steward, who did our cooking. The men cooked amongst themselves by turns.

A small lean-to or shed was fitted up behind our hut, and a fire-place dug out of the bank behind which we were sheltered, and snugly built with stones. A shaft was sunk through the bank down to the fire-place, and acted as a chimney. The lean-to served as the steward's room and cookhouse. I had a bunk, or stretcher, fitted up on one side of our hut, the captain and steward had theirs on the other side, a stove which we manufactured out of an oil can, and a small rough table, filled the third side. Our furniture consisted of the captain's wooden stool, and my empty keg, which served me for nearly four months, as easy chair, rocker and stool of repentance.

The men also managed to rig up some kind of a stove in their hut but had difficulty with a stove pipe.

We soon began to find out that much ingenuity was required to meet the exigencies of life on a desolate island, where there were no shops, and where everything had to be manufactured, and that without tools. At such times necessity is indeed the mother of invention. One brilliant genius who at first got laughed at for his pains, insisted that if he could get the cooper's hoop iron out of the wreck, he could make a good stove pipe by making a number of small hoops well "splayed," i.e. formed with a larger diameter at the lower edge than at the upper, and then stacked one on top of the other, "as high as a church if you like." He had known this plan to operate efficiently on the sealing islands off the Cape of Good Hope.

Our camp was situated at the head of a wide bay, on a narrow isthmus between two mountains, exposed to the southerly winds, but sheltered from all others. The spray from "all the airts that wind can blow," blew clean across from sea to sea, except in calm weather, which was remarkably seldom. Out hut was about fifteen feet from the water's edge at high tide. The outlook was wild and impressive; the almost perpendicular cliffs, the rugged rocks standing far out in the sea, the angry breakers, the ever writhing and glistening tangle of weed. One especially big black rock or island stood opposite our hut, as if on guard. It was in perpetual conflict with the ocean, whose waves broke high in the air, and fell again in cataracts of spray. The wild sea-birds, albatross, stormy petrel, Mother Carey's chickens, and Molly-mawks were in their elements amid the crashing breakers.

There is a pleasure in the pathless woods,
There is a rapture in the lonely shore
There is society where none intrudes
By the deep sea, and music in its roar.[120]
                                        Byron.

Soon after our settlement on the island, a deputation from the crew informed me that as the ship was wrecked, the contract was broken, and that they did not consider themselves under orders any more. To this I at once agreed, advising them at the same time to make the best of the position. The wisest course was to work amicably together for the general welfare, not to be selfish, however great the temptation, and to get as much fun and enjoyment as possible while on the island. We had all looked death in the face several times on the *Bencleugh,* and we were not going to quarrel, but to get along like a band of brothers. I told them that the *Friendship,* might arrive any day, and take us all back to New Zealand. The *Friendship* was another schooner belonging to my brother and myself, but which was under charter to another firm. She had left New Zealand at the same time as the *Bencleugh.*

The unemployment difficulty was amicably settled later on, when the men's natural instinct to do something had asserted itself. It was agreed that double the rates at which they "signed on" should be paid to them, on all oil and skins obtained while on the island.

---

120   There is Pleasure in the Pathless Woods: From Childe Harold's Pilgrimage, by
       Lord Byron.

CHAPTER XXIII

A WALK ROUND THE ISLAND

THE weather now began to improve, the sun shone out, and the fog lifted from the hill-tops, showing the nakedness of the island. There was not a tree or shrub of any kind, but just a fringe of grass growing half-way up the hills, above which there was no visible vegetation whatever.

Two of our men with exploring instincts started one morning to walk round the island. They only took a few biscuits in their pockets, expecting to be back at night. On the third day they had not returned, and fearing that some accident had happened, I set off with two of the hands to search the island for them, taking three days provisions with us, and also my gun. We found that the tracks of the explorers indicated that they had kept on the beach as much as possible, only taking to the hills when they could not pass under the cliffs on account of the sea. So we had no great difficulty in following them.

In coming down a precipitous cliff the canvas which was intended for our tent became detached from Cockney's swag, and was not missed till long after. We decided not to go back to look for it consequently the next four nights we had to "sleep out" without any covering. A sheltered corner was usually found, and a quantity of grass tussocks were collected to make a break-wind. The bright moonlight, and the novelty of the situation kept me from sleeping much. The frost towards morning was usually sharp.

The day after we started I shot two brace of small green parakeets. How they came to Macquarie Island is a mystery, as they are tropical birds. There appeared to be great numbers of them. We roasted them on sticks on our fire of driftwood, and found them a delicious accompaniment to our biscuits and coffee.

The travelling continued to be tolerably easy, being mostly on the beaches. In rounding the rocks we often got thoroughly wet, but we trudged on notwithstanding. We came across a Molly-mawk's nest, with one egg, which we divided between us raw. It was voted first-rate, but hunger makes good sauce!

At last we reached the extreme southern end of the island, a long tongue of level land (about the only level land on the island), jutting out towards the sea. Away beyond and extending many miles out to sea were a series of rocky islets and sunken reefs on which the seas were breaking heavily.

An extraordinary spectacle here presented itself; a herd of about thirty sea-elephants were found resting and sleeping amongst the grassy tussocks, some of them of very large size, and apparently centuries old. Our presence did not appear to disturb or alarm them in the slightest. As they gazed at us out of their large, beautiful eyes, they seemed to express themselves, saying, "Who, and what in the name of Father Neptune are you?" Occasionally they would make a long bark or a roar, which resembled the roar of a lion. They are great clumsy-looking animals on shore, but their tusks, whiskers, and inflated proboscis, give them a very formidable appearance. This appearance is still more evident when they are reared on their hind quarters, for defensive purposes. They seem smarter than kittens when at play in the surf.

When I first saw these sea-elephants in deep water at sea, I very well understood the sailors' belief in mermaids. The cows are much smaller than the bulls, and almost flesh coloured.

Two other nests were found, with an egg in each. These were hard boiled and sliced, and I need hardly say appreciated. It was getting towards the end of the winter, and the birds were just beginning to lay.

The travelling on the west side of the island was much more precipitous and difficult, and we were obliged to climb the cliffs in several places. This was difficult work at times, as we had to cut with our sheath knives places for our hands and feet, and occasionally we had to haul each other up with the swag lines. Baker who was the heaviest man and came last, had a narrow escape of a bad fall, as the ledge on which he stood gave way from under him, and crashed to the beach below. Fortunately he caught the end of the swag line, although not a moment too soon, and so escaped.

In one of these rough scrambles, our meat tin, which served as our billy, or kettle, disappeared, leaving us with only the handle. We tried the coffee with cold water, but it was no good; we also tried to eat it, but that was equally unsuccessful.

At the end of the third day the provisions we had taken with us from the camp were all finished. I shot some parakeets, and occasionally we were successful in knocking them over with stones, but we could never get enough of them to satisfy our hunger, and not another egg was found for the remainder of our journey.

We were now obliged to travel along the top of the cliffs, where the snow was often knee deep, and at times in dense fog. At last we arrived at Caroline Harbour, and on reaching the beach the sun shone out and the fog disappeared, which put us into better spirits. Caroline Harbour is a natural and fairly well protected boat harbour; a schooner might even anchor there in very fine weather only. We found on the beach the wreckage of a large ship. Judging from the old build of the blocks and the immense hawser pipes, she had evidently belonged to the period of the rope cables. We also found a quantity of copper and sheet lead, stacked above the high-water mark, and discovered a large cave which had been used as a dwelling place. I would gladly have spent more time exploring, but we did not know how far we had yet to travel, and a search for food was imperative.

The cliffs prevented us keeping on the beach, and we were obliged once more to take to the hills. What with the steepness of the slopes, grassy tussocks and soft snow, the travelling was most fatiguing.

When we camped that night we simply burrowed in a hollow in the ground, and had one single blanket and a canvas one to cover the three or us. We could see the place where we had started from in the morning, not more than three miles distant as the crow flies, but the physical fatigue of the journey had been something extraordinary and it proved our worst day's travelling. During the night it came on to rain and the ground became soaked and sodden. We ourselves did not escape dry.

On the fourth day we got down to flat, boggy ground, and were cheered by finding, like Robinson Crusoe, human tracks, which proved to be those of the men we were in search of. We were feeling the want of food, and the sight of a covey of wild ducks set me running to get a shot at them. I had not run far when I sank up to my knees in a bog. Before I could be extricated the birds had flown, much to our disappointment.

Late in the afternoon we succeeded in killing a young sea-elephant, and without delay made a fire of driftwood and roasted the meat. It tasted delicious though the only accompaniment we had was cold water. We ate sparingly that night, not being sure how it would agree with us. Next morning we felt much better, and did not hesitate to have a good "tuck in." I was reminded of the Esquimaux practice of cutting a hole in a big chunk of the flesh, through which a man inserted his head, and so carried it on his shoulders. We did not adopt this plan, but we cut off a quantity of steaks for future meals. What with our dirty, tattered clothes and shoes, and our burden of meat, we might have passed for cannibals.

On rounding a headland we were delighted to see the outlying islets, the Judge and Clerks, at the Northern end of the island, and recognised we were not very far from the camp. We found hereabouts a ship's figurehead (a large eagle), quite a number of logs, of what we supposed to be Australian red cedar, and some sperm candles, which had been washed ashore with other wreckage.

Finally on the fifth day, we reached the camp, having completed a circuit of the island. We found that the wanderers had arrived three days previously, and had fared worse than we did, being obliged to live on parakeets, which they ate raw. One of the men was for a time so overcome by the hardships of the journey, that he was completely off his head. We received a boisterous welcome from our comrades. That evening we had a great feast of elephant-seal stew, bread and tea. Never having been so thoroughly hungry before in my life, I thoroughly enjoyed it, in spite of the rough and unattractive surroundings of the camp. The shelter and warmth of the cabin after the hard experience of the five days previous was very welcome.

CHAPTER XXIV

SAIL HO! ABANDONED

THE arrival of the *Friendship* -- 14 days after our shipwreck -- made no small excitement at the camp. A long steer oar was erected opposite the opening in the reef, and the *Friendship's* five-oared whale boat got through in fine style, and was quickly run up the beach by willing hands.

It was suggested that Captain Sewell should land his party at the southern end of our island, where they could engage in sealing, and then return and take our three invalids and as many more of the *Bencleugh* party as might be arranged home to Port Chalmers.

I watched the schooner's departure, with strange misgivings, till long after she was hull down, and almost out of sight. She had been running with a fair wind, and her two masts appeared as one. I then observed that she had quite altered her course, for the two masts were seen wide apart. She has changed her tack and is off to Emerald Island, I immediately concluded, and we were abandoned meantime.

The position of Emerald Island is given in the old charts as about two days' sail from Macquarie in a south-east direction. It has now been proved that the island does not really exist; both the *Friendship* and the *Bencleugh* having sailed over the position marked on the charts several times.

The attraction of Emerald Isle was this, that never having been fished, it was supposed that it would be very rich in fur seals, elephant-seals, or sea-lions. The first party that landed on Macquarie were said to have taken an enormous quantity of very valuable fur skins. After the *Friendship* had reported the non-existence it was then blotted out from all new Admiralty charts. In 1909 Sir Ernest Shackleton sailed over the same position in the *Nimrod*.

A continuance of winter westerly gales drove the *Friendship* a long way to the east and north. Captain Sewell then bore up for Port Chalmers and reported our demise. The schooner was immediately fitted out again, and despatched for our relief. When she arrived once more at Macquarie, nearly four months had elapsed since the wreck of the *Bencleugh*. Meanwhile our huts had been made as comfortable as possible. The devices of our handy men were wonderfully effective and ingenious. The stove in our cabin was made from a five-gallon oil drum. The lamp was made from a preserved meat tin. The burner was a piece of tin cut the shape of a four-pointed star, the four points resting on four pieces of cork, which floated on the surface of the elephant oil. A hole cut in the centre of the star held the wick, which was made of a fragment of moleskin trousers.[121]

The light from our lamp was quite brilliant. All the men had suits of clothes made from the *Bencleugh's* sails, the construction and the elegance of fit being quite amazing: but sailors are generally

---

121   JIT: To what varied uses moleskin trousers have been adapted! See Chapter V.

good tailors. The buttons were made of various shapes in wood, or of Turk's heads or crown knots.

I was the only one who till the end had tweed clothes. My only coat had been washed ashore through the ribs of the schooner. It had been much torn, but carefully repaired with twine made by teasing out the threads of the canvas. Thread and needles not being "in season" there was a great run on the two salved sail needles!

We were badly off for boots and shoes, but moccasins were made from sea-leopards' skins, and after a few trials were made quite smart and comfortable. I had been wearing a pair of rubber knee-boots when the ship was wrecked, but kicked them off when in the rigging, expecting every moment to have to attempt to swim. One of the boots was washed ashore first, and the other one a fortnight afterwards.

Our woollen socks were very soon worn out; a handful of dried grass was used as a substitute, being placed inside the boots. This with the friction accompanying walking, kept the feet wonderfully warm and dry.

We were soon reduced to two stumps of clay pipes. These were recognised as common property, and were seldom allowed to cool, tobacco being our most abundant possession. The pipe difficulty was overcome later, by taking the back teeth of young sea-elephants, which made good pipe bowls, and then inserting the quill of an albatross feather. This acted for the shank, and the new pipe was voted a triumphant success.

As regards fire-arms, the rifle was found to be hopelessly injured. The bag of bullets and the bullet moulds for the two double-barrelled guns were lost. We, however, made bullet moulds from pieces of the cooper's chalk, and sheet lead was stripped from the wreck and melted in our frying pan (an old shovel!) into the moulds. The resultant bullets were far from mathematically true, but they answered the purpose.

The skull of a sea-elephant is of great thickness, and we found it necessary, in order to reach the brain with fatal results, to load with double charges of powder and ball, and then to fire at the eye or through the roof of the open mouth. Our guns were the now old-fashioned muzzle-loading percussion-cap guns, and the ramrod was made from the handle of a whaling lance, but how to make a nipple key, to unscrew the percussion nipple, was a problem that puzzled us for many a day. The only way to withdraw the charges when the guns choked, which on account of the snow and the rain often happened, was to put the disconnected barrels in the fire, pointing up the chimney, and allow them to explode. This was dangerous for our kitchen and drawing-room, as well as life and limb. It was necessary to make the nipple key or wrench with parallel sides, to unscrew the nipples. The only available tool was a three-cornered file, too large to be of any use. At last it occurred to me to make a ward file out of a sailor's sheath knife. So the three cornered file was used to cut notches on the back of the sheath knife, and very soon a file was made, and with this a very efficient nipple key was made, and was in successful use all the time we were on the island. Owing to the heavy work my gun was doing, the stock was strengthened by frapping it around with copper wire. On one occasion, in order to get a good effective shot at a large sea-elephant which was lying fast asleep among the long tussocky grass, I pressed down on a tussock with the butt end of the gun, and unfortunately almost broke the stock in two pieces. I then fired, but owing to the position of the elephant, the only effect of my shot was to wake him up and make him very angry. The stock of the gun was now in two pieces; the second barrel was loaded but it was evidently unsafe to fire. I regretted that I had disturbed his majesty, for he was a pretty large one, over twenty feet from tip to tip. When, however, I saw he was about to escape, I could not resist the temptation of a second shot. Clapping the shattered pieces of the gun together and grasping them firmly with my hand in front of the sights, I fired at the roof of his open mouth and instantly the huge animal fell dead. Alas my poor gun! And my poor fingers. The barrels were spinning high in the air, the stock went in three pieces and my fingers "dirled" for days afterwards.

The gun was too precious to abandon, so the fragments were carefully collected, and with the aid of one of our handy men, it was reconstructed after a fashion, being spliced and fished and frapped after the most approved nautical methods. The steel spring of the trigger was broken. As a substitute a copper nail was driven through a lead bullet and made to work up and down through a hole bored from the top of the stock, and acting by gravitation as a pawl, served as an excellent substitute. The whole arrangement looked rather comical, but till we left the island the gun proved quite effective, so long as it was fired horizontally, or nearly so.

Our percussion caps having been exhausted, revolver caps were made to answer in their stead, by being carefully split.

When Enderby's party visited the island about 1830, they built three sets of try works on different parts of the coast, consisting of large try pots,[122] or boilers and furnaces. These we were able to put into efficient order, and they served us for boiling down the blubber

---

122   A try pot is a metallic pot used on a whaler or on shore to render whale oil from blubber. https://www.merriam-webster.com/dictionary/try-pot

of the seals, etc. This was very fortunate, as our own try pots had been lost with the ship, and but for these, we should have had little or no employment. Man is made for work, and unemployment is the curse of every sphere of life, from the guttersnipe to dukes and earls.

We found a small try pot which had been built into the bank bottom up, and used for an oven. Our own cooking experiences were novel. Most of our scones were fried on an old broken shovel. Our damper was simply dough covered at night with hot wood ashes; it was found to be thoroughly cooked in the morning. Our bread was chiefly in the form of pancakes, which we must have eaten by the thousand. We had come across three large bottles of lime-juice and a quantity of liquid sugar in the bottom of a barrel, which had been left in the hut by the previous occupants. Both the lime-juice and the sugar were invaluable. The lime-juice may have also served to keep away scurvy, as we had no vegetables except Macquarie "cabbage," a combination of parsnip and cabbage, and not particularly palatable.

After the first fortnight, when we had rested and recruited somewhat, our health was on the whole excellent. So much for the simple life. When the penguin eggs began to arrive, and the men commenced to work among oil, they fattened visibly. Choice cuts of sea-elephant (their tongues are excellent), penguin liver, and kidney stew, and various kinds of birds "a la mode," all contributed to our meals. The elephant flesh is darker in colour than cow beef, guaranteed free from tuberculosis, and not at all fishy flavoured.

The intense cold, with hunger for a relish, gave us excellent appetites; as "Glasgow" remarked, we had "Aw the luxuries of the Sawt Market." Epicurean tastes quickly disappear at such times.

The favourite stroll of the men was along the beach where the wreck lay, and an eager lookout was kept for anything that might be washed ashore. After a south-easterly gale especially valuable finds were sometimes made. On one occasion about eight inches of an American axe handle was observed standing perpendicular among the shingle in the surf. It was recovered with difficulty, and at the cost of a thorough soaking. This proved to be the most valuable find for cutting firewood and other purposes.

On another occasion I met one of the men in a great state of excitement carrying aloft what seemed to be a cabbage stalk, or "kale runt." It proved however to be something much more valuable, viz., a bar of soap. It had been entangled and scored by the sea-weed and shingle, so as to be beyond recognition at first sight as soap. It was esteemed a great prize while it lasted. Later on some genius in the crew, with some alongshore experience, contrived to manufacture a kind of lye, made from wood ashes and oil, which served as a substitute for soap.

A paint can was another memorable find. It was immediately utilised for a coffee pot, as we had scarcely any cooking utensils. After breakfast all three in the cabin were seized with violent sickness and diarrhoea. It was then discovered that the paint-drum had contained dry red lead. The boiling water had expelled quite a quantity of it from the folds of the iron, with the result that we were all seriously poisoned, and from the effects of this we were a long time in recovering. I have since been told that if we had not had such a large dose of the poison, and so become very sick, it might have proved fatal.

Our whale-boat, which with the davits had been swept away before the vessel struck, we found washed up on the beach, the two sides being split apart, and only attached at the keel. Our intention was to endeavour to make her fit for use, but before an opportunity occurred, a squall carried the boat about half a mile away and smashed her all to bits. This was a matter of much regret, but we were glad of the broken planking and copper nails for repairing the dinghy, which we managed to cobble up and make almost watertight.

We also found on the island a ship's boat with the bottom stove in. This, too, we were able to repair, and it came in useful for coasting when the weather permitted, which was very seldom.[123]

Oars were the next difficulty. Most of those salved were broken in two pieces. They had become entangled in the seaweed and shingle, and then the incoming rollers had broken them across. So we had to splice them as best we could, and then frap them round with hoop iron. Then they served the purpose efficiently.

On one of our sea trips when off the Nuggets, we narrowly escaped being blown out to sea by a fierce squall. We had almost given up hope, when we were able to make up our leeway and reached the landing thoroughly exhausted.

On another occasion, when coasting, we were tempted by the sight of a group of elephants to beach the boat through a rather dangerous surf. We killed and flensed the animals and loaded up the boat with blubber. After launching, she was caught by the breakers and thrown on a rock, smashing the quarter and six of the planks. We managed to scramble ashore and hauled her up again. The hands then decided to abandon the boat and walk to the camp. To repair it was declared impossible, for we had no nails, boards, oakum, or tools, except one small axe. I proposed, however, that an attempt should be made. At my suggestion we prised off the lining boards in the floor of the boat, with the nails attached, and after covering

---

123   JIT: The weather was very stormy nearly the whole time; we never could count on the continuance of fine weather for more than half a day.

the damaged pieces with elephant skin, nailed the boards over all, and succeeded in making a nearly watertight repair. Once more necessity was the mother of invention.

Alas! Our fine contrivance did not prevent the utter destruction of the boat. We were scarcely clear of the breakers when we were caught by a big sea and violently dashed on the rocks. The boat was smashed all to pieces. Fortunately we reached the shore in safety, and betook ourselves to the hills and beaches to reach the camp.

The behaviour of the crew throughout was, all things considered, excellent. They were carefully selected men, being shipped with a view to rough, dangerous work. They were strong manly fellows.

One had fought all through the American war, sometimes Federal, sometimes Confederate; he didn't care which. As he expressed it: "The dollars advanced on joining a new regiment, and plunder was my dart." Others had been repeatedly shipwrecked, had lived among savages, and could tell of strange scenes and adventures.

One of the crew very nearly killed me, though quite by accident. This was how it happened. One Sunday he called at the hut door, and asked if he might have the use of the gun as there was a large elephant-seal on the beach. He would kill it and the flensing could stand till Monday. I handed my rickety loaded gun to him, rather carelessly, perhaps, when it immediately exploded, the charge passing within a few inches of my body, through a portion of the Bible which lay on the shelf, and out through the wall of the hut.

On the whole there was little quarrelling or fighting; all working harmoniously together. Drink and money, the causes of most quarrels in civilised countries, were absent, and that may account for the good fellowship which pervaded the camp. If so it has a lesson for this age of industrial strife. To work happily together for the common good is better than selfish competition. The accumulation of millions of money is a paltry object in life, when the greater work of cultivating the happiness of millions of men, women and children is considered. "Thy Kingdom come" is worth working for, living for, praying for, and dying for.

"Mankind is destined to have one religion, and one universal truth. Science will spread slowly, but surely, and the scientific world conception is leading the way to the religion of truth – the one truth, the one religion, the one moral end, and the one Eternal God who exists for ever."[124]

Our Bible readings were held every evening, with no attempt at preaching. There were only two books on the island, *viz.*, a Bible, and a tattered volume of the "Sunday at Home," with two fragments of old hymn books. The last named we found in the huts. The reading of the Scriptures, the best of all literature, was always listened to most reverently. Songs and hymn-singing, and two roughly-made draught boards, were the chief recreations, and helped to pass the long nights. In the choruses what was lacking in quality of tone was made up for in volume, enough at times to lift the roof. To hear the men sing: –

> *"Home at last they labour done,*
> *Home at last the victory won,"*

was something to be remembered.

The north-eastern extremity of the island consisted of a high, hilly peninsula. This was often climbed to look out for passing vessels, but none were ever seen. A peculiarity of this hill is that it

---

124　　　Count Kaneko Kentarō (1853-1942). Japanese statesman, diplomat and scholar.

was always trembling. When one lies flat on the ground, the vibration is unmistakable. Possibly it is caused by the heavy seas thundering at the base of the cliffs. The whole peninsula is honeycombed with the nesting burrows of the mutton-birds. There was a curious blow-hole in the hill near the top, which was connected with a series of caves on the beach.

Looking down over the perpendicular cliffs, at the extremity of this hill, a magnificent sea-scape was presented to the gaze.

So tremendous are the crashing and undermining assaults of the western seas on Macquarie and the Auckland Islands, that a heavy storm causes the exposed localities to be altered so much almost beyond recognition.

The poet Björnson has observed that, "It is in the neighbourhood of death that religion is born." Goethe's idea of the birth and development of religion (if I rightly remember it) seems more correct and genuine, first the beginning to wonder, then to admire, and afterwards to reverence, first what is around, secondly, what is above, and lastly what is beneath, even the criminal on the gallows or the worm on the footpath.

King David sets forth his views, in the nineteenth Psalm saying, "The heavens declare God's glory, and the firmament showeth forth," etc., and asserting that all Nature cries aloud, in language unmistakable, and showing only in hearkening to and obeying the precepts and laws of God is there true religion.

Christ taught the Kingdom (or reign) of God within, to love one another, and that *Love* was the fulfilling of all law, and the golden rule to do unto others as we would they should do unto us.

And the Prophets of old taught, that to do justly, to love mercy (or kindness), and to walk humbly, was all that the Lord required of us, the sum of all teaching being contained in the one word, *Righteousness.*

Notwithstanding that the Tammany men of New York boast that they "have knocked truth and righteousness into a cocked hat," yet truth and righteousness still remain, and are the grand aim of all those who are working for the progress and uplift of humanity.

Thinking occasionally on such subjects on the mountain top, or by the seashore, with the great starry vault of heaven overhead, one cannot help coming to the conclusion, that Nature is God's Bible, that every page is open for us to read, so as to understand the works, the wonders, and the words of God. He is always the all-pervading "God beautiful," whose works and ways and doings are beautiful, beneficent, and good."

CHAPTER XXV

PENGUIN, AND OTHER BIRDS. RESCUE AND ARRIVAL HOME

COLLECTING eggs, coopering the oil barrels, stalking, killing sea-beasts, boiling oil, and repairing clothes and shoes, kept all hands fairly busy. When our provisions began to run short, they were carefully doled out, and anything like waste prevented. We collected nearly a hogshead of penguin eggs, and preserved them in salt, in case of necessity.

Our very good friends, the penguins, deserve a chapter to themselves, as we were very much indebted to them for sustenance and health, for thousands of eggs, and many a savoury stew. There were very few on the island at first, but in the beginning of September they arrived in tens of thousands. They swim so rapidly that from a boat nothing is to be seen but a flash of light. In certain days where they landed to lay their eggs, a most extraordinary and interesting spectacle was presented. After shooting through the breakers, they landed on the beach, forming themselves into a wedge-shaped column, and approached us in a most inquisitive, yet quite friendly manner.

We noticed four varieties, the golden-necked Emperor, or King Penguin, measuring four feet in height, the Royal, the Rock-Hopper, and the Victoria.

Bencleugh valley during the breeding season is also a most wonderful place to visit. From the water's edge to the tops of the hills is one living mass of penguins, seemingly all in a state of the greatest excitement and happiness. Most of them continue sitting on the one or two eggs, and jabber away in noisy fashion. We made a rough estimate of the acreage, and of the number of penguins to the square yard and concluded that there were in sight no less than 180,000.

The young penguins looked particularly quaint and ludicrous. They were grey and furry and somewhat like animated chinchilla ladies' muffs. There were also on the island, albatross, mutton-birds, vultures, Molly-mawks, Mother Carey's chickens, small bright green parakeets, etc.

When in the neighbourhood of the vultures' nests we had to defend ourselves from their attacks. They kept continually swooping down from aloft with the speed of an arrow, to within a foot of our heads. They were most voracious birds, and they pick clean the carcasses of the sea-elephants, gorging themselves to such an extent that they have difficulty in flying away after their meal. Their eyesight must be extraordinarily keen, for immediately a sea-elephant is attacked, they swoop down in great numbers with incredible speed and boldness. As an instance of their rapacity, a small whale was cast up on the beach one evening, and on the following morning nothing but the skeleton remained.

The hills and cliffs at the northern extremity of the island are completely honey-combed with mutton-bird nests. The birds are fairly good eating, but not equal to the little green parakeets, which we looked upon as a real delicacy.

There were no rabbits at the time of our stay on the island. They were however, imported by Elder and Co., who succeeded our party, and since then they have increased enormously.[125]

News from the outside world was, of course, absolutely nil, though there was much speculation as to what was going on there. The report of some wreckage, a booby hutch and a beer bottle, having been seen among the breakers, made quite a stir in our little kingdom. We found a broken mast which is supposed to have belonged to the Leith ship *Countess of Seafield,* and the party who succeeded us found on the beach a bell, which had been rolled among the shingle by the waves for forty long years. The lettering *Countess of Seafield,* was just decipherable. It was taken to Port Chalmers, and sent from there as a present to Captain Allan, at Newcastle, N.S.W., for he had been master of the ill-fated ship.

The *Friendship,* after leaving Macquarie and cruising about in search of the non-existent Emerald Island, was driven by continuous gales far to the eastward, and at long last arrived near the coast of New Zealand, bore up for Port Chalmers, and reported the wreck of the *Bencleugh.* She was immediately dispatched back to Macquarie for our relief. Her arrival was hailed with great delight. Immediately all were in a state of cheerful and boisterous excitement.

We had made fifteen tons of oil. This was speedily rolled down

---

125   In March 2014, after an eradication programme, it was announced there had been no confirmed sightings of ship rats or house mice since July 2011 and no confirmed sightings of rabbits since December 2011. https://www.dcceew.gov.au/sites/default/files/env/pages/f47bc054-b46d-40f2-85a5-7825525bfb48/files/fs-macquarie-island.pdf

to the water's edge; rope beckets[126] were fixed in simple sailor fashion to the hoops of the barrels, for convenience in floating and towing them. They were then rolled and pushed into the surf, towed alongside the schooner, and hoisted on board. The men got wet up to the neck in the launching, but they were homeward bound, and worked most willingly.

I had very carefully preserved a fine specimen of a sea-elephant, twenty-two feet in length, intended for the Dunedin Museum. The skin had been put into salt in a large oil barrel. We arranged for it to be taken aboard in the last boat, with Captain Bezer, Mr. Low, the mate, and myself. It being impossible to lift the cask, the boat was turned over on its broadside, the gunwale under the bilge of the barrel, which was then rolled into the bottom and the boat righted. We were then dismayed to notice one of the bottom planks had been forced in, so that there was a hole in the bottom of the boat big enough to admit a man's hand. The plank, however, sprang back into its place again, and we decided to risk it, as it was now getting dusk, and so the boat was launched through the surf.

Fate, however, was against us, for a dense fog set in, making it impossible to find the *Friendship*. We rowed out in the direction of the schooner, and hallooed together our very loudest, but no reply came.

We then decided to stand in for the shore, and guided only by the direction of the wind, and the roll of the sea, we were fortunate enough to make out the loom of the land, then to hear and to see the breakers.

To attempt to land would have been disastrous, as the rocks were all about us, and it was now quite dark, so we headed down

126   A loop of rope or similar device for securing items on ships.

the coast, to a comparatively sheltered little bay, and after waiting for a smooth, worked the boat in through the breakers, and struck the beach heavily. The next sea filled the boat, and turned her broadside on, but we managed to scramble ashore safely. Much to my chagrin, we found the cask containing my beautiful elephant skin had disappeared amidst the white breakers.

After a long, weary tramp, we at last reached our old camp, and slept there till daylight, when the *Friendship's* boat's crew came on shore. They were both surprised and delighted to find us all safe. Very speedily we got on board, weighed anchor, and set sail. We were not sorry to leave the wreck-strewn shores of this lone, tempestuous island, where we had been for nearly four months, the *furthest south* inhabitants on the planet.

The wind not being favourable, we made a course which we expected would take us round the north end of the Auckland Islands. What was out astonishment when day broke to find land close to our port beam. This turned out to be Disappointment Island, the most southerly of the Auckland Island group. The position was perfectly inexplicable, considering the course by compass that had been steered.

It was then discovered that a large pair of steel scissors, which had been used for trimming the binnacle lamp[127], had fallen into the case, close to the compass, and deviated the needle some two to three points. This explained matters.

If the wind had not been contrary, in all likelihood we should have struck the precipitous cliffs of the Aucklands during the night

---

127   A binnacle is the housing for a ship's compass. The idea behind a binnacle is to counter the magnetic deviation caused by the ship being made of iron so that the compass can point to magnetic north. Metals that were used to construct binnacles were required to be non-ferrous (containing no iron) such as brass.

and added another to the long list of "never-heard-of-mores."[128]

I have now "coiled up my ropes" and quietly settled in Bonny Scotland in the Perthshire town[129] that is often called "Rest and be thankful" in a quiet eddy of the turbulent eddy of my life —— waiting for the next flood to carry me out "across the bar."

Never again will I have the opportunity of saying a helpful word to my patient readers and the friends for whom my true story has been written, so in bidding adieu I would remark that after close on seventy years' experience during which I have blundered and wandered, in my earnest search for truth, and for solution of the problem and mystery of life from Calvinism to Free Thought and Confucianism with various stages between, that the conclusion I have come back is this, that *to fear God and keep His commandments* is the best, wisest and happiest rule of life and conduct; this means harmony with Nature, full development, rest, peace, satisfaction, obedience to the Golden Rule, to do unto others as ye would have that others should do unto you. It means in one word *Love,* with victory over all the storms if life, its sunshine, and its calm.

---

128   JIT: The Auckland Islands have been the perfect graveyard for ships in the Australian and Home trade, among which were the Grafton, the Invercauld with the loss of 22 lives, the Derry Castle with 15, and the General Grant 73. The survivors endured great hardships and lived chiefly on seals and sea birds. The General Grant got in under overhanging rocks which fell on her decks. She had a very large quantity of bullion on board, and many expeditions have attempted to salve it, but all unsuccessfully.

129   Blairgowrie.

John Sen Inches Thomson: "The sailor home from the sea."

BIBLIOGRAPHY

BOOKS:

1. Captain William Thomson: His Life, by Shirley Cameron. 2009

2. Ben Line: Fleet History and Short History, by Graeme Somner. World Ship Society. 1980

3. The Penguin History of New Zealand, by Michael King. Penguin Books. 2003

4. Contributions to the Early History of New Zealand [Otago], by Thomas Moreland Hocken. Sampson Low, Marston and Company. London EC. 1898

5. New Zealand or Ao-Teā-Roa. [The Long Bright World], by James Cowan. New Zealand Government Department of Tourist and Health Resorts. 1908.

6. The Port of Otago, by A. H. McLintock. Whitcombe and Tombs Limited. 1951.

7. Ask That Mountain: The Story of Parihaka, by Dick Scott. Penguin Group. 1975.

8. Tamate: The Life Story of James Chalmers, by Richard Lovett. The Religious Tract Society, London. 1908.

9. Te Wai Pounamu: The Greenstone Island. A History of the Southern Māori during the European Colonization of New Zealand, by H. C. Evison. Aoraki Press. 1993.

10. The Welcome of Strangers. An Ethnohistory of Southern Māori 1650-1850, by Atholl Anderson. Otago University Press. 1998.

11. Diggers, Hatters and Whores. The Story of the New Zealand Gold Rushes, by Steven Eldred-Grigg. Random House New Zealand.

12. Early Gold Discoveries in Otago by Vincent Pyke M.H.R. Otago Daily Times and Witness Newspapers Company, Ltd. 1887.

13. Ngāi Tahu, A Migration History. The Carrington Text. Edited by Te Maire Tau and Atholl Anderson. Bridget Williams Books. 2008.

14. Colonialism: A Moral Reckoning by Nigel Biggar. William Collins. Harper Collins*Publishing.* 2023.

15. Replenishing the Earth: The Settler Revolution and the Rise of the Anglo-World, 1783 -1939, by James Belich. Oxford University Press, 2008.

ONLINE SOURCES:
1. https://teara.govt.nz
2. https://en.wikipedia.org/wiki
3. https://nzetc.victoria.ac.nz
4. https://www.dcceew.gov.au
5. https://www.snowroads.com/history/places/cargill-s-leap

6. https://www.iponz.govt.nz
7. https://www.ambergris.fr/information.html
8. http://www.immigration.gov.pn/history
9. https://wrecksite.eu/wreck.aspx?146195
10. https://nzhistory.govt.nz
11. https://www.wikitree.com/wiki
12. https://www.ancestry.com
13. https://www.merriam-webster.com/dictionary
14. https://www.dcceew.gov.au/sites
15. https://natlib.govt.nz/records
16. http://www.bmimages.com
17. https://www.alamy.com/
18. https://scotlandspeople.gov.uk
19. http://www.toitusm.com

ACKNOWLEDGEMENTS

THANK-YOU to those who have so willingly helped in this endeavour. In particular, this book would not have been possible without the help and resources of Blair Thomson, my third cousin through our mutual great (gt) grandfather, John's brother, Andrew Thomson. You have a scholarly knowledge of the family built up over many years and your willingness to share family information and photographs was most gratifying. Thanks also to my cousin Jane Batchelor, and sister Prue Thomson for their help with information and for providing photographs of family paintings.

I am grateful to the staff at the National Library of New Zealand, Scotland's People, the Hocken Library, Toitu: The Otago Early Settlers Museum, the Port Chalmers Maritime Museum and the British Library for their help and assistance finding material and sourcing illustrations. Paul Diamond and Sean Brosnahan, thank you for your expert advice.

Thank you to Lucia Zanmonti for your help getting photographs and illustrations into a publishable condition.

Cover Painting: Port Chalmers, 1864: Attributed to Captain Thomas Robertson (1819-1873), marine artist. Thomson family painting in the collection of Dr Jane Batchelor, Christchurch.

Inside Front Cover: Map of Otago Harbour: Inside cover illustration: The Port of Otago: McLintock. 1951.

Inside Back Cover: Map of Sea Routes (1908): Taken from: New Zealand or Ao-Teā-Roa. [The Long Bright World], by James Cowan. New Zealand Government Department of Tourist and Health Resorts. 1908.

Cover and book design by Amanda Sutcliffe.

Rosy Fenwicke.
(Photograph: Lucia Zanmotti)

Rosy Fenwicke is a full time writer and publisher, based in Martinborough, New Zealand. Her fiction works include; Books 1-4 The Euphemia Sage Chronicles, Death Actually, and Cold Wallet. In Practice: The Lives of New Zealand Women Doctors in the 21st Century, a non-fiction work was published in 2004 by Random House NZ.

For more information: www.rosyfenwickeauthor.com